Adopting a UDL Att Academia

Adopting a UDL Attitude within Academia bridges the gap between the theory and practice of UDL (Universal Design for Learning). It guides the reader through the origins of the development of UDL as an innovative way of thinking about inclusion and the evolution of this theory into practice, as it explores UDL and its relevance beyond the classroom.

Including reader-friendly descriptions and case studies supplemented with international research, this book allows the reader to think and see through a UDL lens, ultimately emphasising their part in the inclusion agenda. From the outset this book shares the attitude necessary to promote UDL and inclusion across higher education and addresses some of the most common questions:

- Is this a scientific theory or just a new practice, and why is it important?
- How can I be more inclusive in my current practice?
- Is it sustainable and how do I ensure I'm implementing it correctly?

The book will have a broad appeal and is essential reading for anyone looking to understand and implement UDL across their learning environment – be it a university or any education institution.

Mary Quirke is a qualified career guidance counsellor with a passion and knowledge about inclusion in education due to her active engagement with learners, teachers, and employers while also actively engaging with UDL across practice and policy. She is completing a Ph.D based in the School of Education at Trinity College Dublin, Ireland.

Conor Mc Guckin is an Associate Professor of Educational Psychology in the School of Education, Trinity College Dublin, Ireland.

Patricia McCarthy is Visiting Research Fellow in the School of Education, Trinity College Dublin, Ireland.

"This is a must read for anyone interested in equality, diversity, and inclusion in education and wider society. This is a modern classic – pioneering and refreshing."

Professor Michael Shevlin, Professor in Inclusive Education, School of Education, Trinity College Dublin, Ireland

"This book shows how to move beyond our individual efforts to create systemic, at-scale methods for making inclusion 'everyone's business' in higher education: in community colleges, trade schools, technical schools, further education, four-year colleges, and universities. I strongly recommend *Adopting a UDL Attitude* to campus and program leaders and practitioners everywhere."

Thomas J. Tobin, author of *Reach Everyone, Teach Everyone: UDL in Higher Education* – PhD, MSLS, PMP, MOT, CPACC, University of Wisconsin-Madison, USA

"This important volume raises important questions and highlights a gap in the current literature on Universal Design for Learning [...] There is no doubt that this volume will be of benefit at many levels."

Fred Fovet is an academic, researcher, consultant and UDL & Inclusion specialist, UDL and Inclusion scholar and researcher (K-12 and post-secondary) and is currently Assistant Professor at the Thompson Rivers University, Kamloops, British Columbia, Canada

"It is a very useful guide on the how and, more importantly, the why, of UDL. In its support for inclusive practice for all it should be recommended reading for those involved in teaching and learning at all levels in higher education."

Professor Noirin Hayes, Visiting Professor, School of Education, Trinity College Dublin, Ireland, and Professor Emeritus, Dublin Institute of Technology, Ireland

"While there is much discourse about inclusion in education – across all of our education system – this book sets out how we in higher education can lead the way – with the right attitude!"

Dr Kate Carr-Fanning, Lecturer in Psychology of Education, the School of Education, University of Bristol. Charactered Psychologist with the British Psychological Society (BPS), Fellow of the Higher Education Academy (FHEA)

Adopting a UDL Attitude within Academia

Understanding and Practicing Inclusion Across Higher Education

Mary Quirke, Conor Mc Guckin and Patricia McCarthy

Routledge
Taylor & Francis Group

LONDON AND NEW YORK

Designed cover image: © Getty Images

First published 2024
by Routledge
4 Park Square, Milton Park, Abingdon, Oxon OX14 4RN

and by Routledge
605 Third Avenue, New York, NY 10158

Routledge is an imprint of the Taylor & Francis Group, an informa business

© 2024 Mary Quirke, Conor Mc Guckin and Patricia McCarthy

British Library Cataloguing-in-Publication Data
A catalogue record for this book is available from the British Library

ISBN: 978-0-367-67397-0 (hbk)
ISBN: 978-0-367-68468-6 (pbk)
ISBN: 978-1-003-13767-2 (ebk)

DOI: 10.4324/9781003137672

Typeset in Galliard
by SPi Technologies India Pvt Ltd (Straive)

"For Paul, Eoin, and Sile-Marie" – Mary
"For Karen, Eunan, and Ethan" – Conor
"For my mum Mary, who never doubted my abilities" – Patricia

Contents

Contributors' Profiles

Carrie Archer is PLD Development Officer for the City of Dublin Education and Training Board (CDETB) in Ireland. She is also involved in teacher education for Further Education and Training (FET) educators in a number of higher education institutions in Dublin, most specifically in the areas of diversity and inclusion. Through her varied roles, Carrie aims to encourage, facilitate, promote, and model a strong culture of professional dialogue, learning, and development through each and every action and interaction.

Sean Bracken is Principal Lecturer and Head of Department for Education and Inclusion at the University of Worcester, United Kingdom. He is also a Principal Fellow of the Higher Education Authority. He has worked in a diversity of countries as a primary and secondary teacher, a teacher educator, a lecturer, and an educational project manager and educational policy developer. Sean is a co-founder of the International Collaboratory for Leadership in Universally Designed Education (INCLUDE, 2019) which adopts a research-informed approach to designing inclusive learning spaces and learning outcomes for all learners.

Cristina Devecchi is Associate Professor in Special and Inclusive Education and the Co-lead of the Centre for Education and Research at the University of Northampton, United Kingdom. She leads on the Further, Higher and Adult Education Special Interest Group and has conducted research focusing on issues of inclusion and social justice across all levels of education.

Geraldine Fitzgerald is Subject Librarian for the School of Education and the School of Psychology in Trinity College Dublin, Ireland. Prior to working in TCD, Geraldine worked in a number of special, corporate, and academic libraries in Ireland and Sweden. Geraldine is passionate about improving the user experience of students and has developed a number of digital resources, including tutorials and floor plans to aid wayfinding. She has recently been involved in the TCDSense project to improve the library sensory environment.

Margaret Flood is Assistant Professor in inclusive and special education in Maynooth University, Ireland. Margaret's research interests are in the field of equity, diversity, and inclusive education, Universal Design for Learning (UDL), inclusive policy and curriculum design and enactment, and teacher professional learning for inclusive practices. Margaret has undertaken research with CAST to review the UDL guidelines and, in 2021, was invited to join CAST's Stakeholder Council for UDL Rising to Equity. She is the creator and host of #UDLchatIE on Twitter and the "Talking about All Things Inclusion" podcast.

Andratesha Fritzgerald is an educator, speaker, and the founder/lead consultant of Building Blocks of Brilliance, LLC. Her award-winning book *Antiracism and Universal Design for Learning: Building Expressways to Success* (CAST, 2020) has been a catalyst for UDL to ensure safety and radical inclusion in every learning community. For more information, go to www.buildingblocksofbrilliance.com and @FritzTesha

John Harding has been Head of the Accessibility & Disability Resource Centre (DRC) at the University of Cambridge in the United Kingdom since 2008. He is Adviser to the Board of the National Association of Disability Practitioners (having served previously for five years as Board Director) and was a UK representative on the LINK pan-European inclusion network for three years. John holds a PGCE in Adult Literacy and also holds a postgraduate diploma in teaching and assessing Specific Learning Difficulties, and is currently in the process of completing his doctorate in education at the University of Cambridge. He is also a Fellow of the Royal Society of Arts.

Gloria Kirwan is a Senior Lecturer in the Graduate School of Healthcare Management at the Royal College of Surgeons, Dublin, having previously held appointments in Trinity College Dublin (2000–2018) and Maynooth University (2018–2022), where she was involved in professional social work education. In addition to her professional social work qualifications, Gloria has studied law and social science to Master's level and successfully completed her Ph.D in 2017. Gloria is currently Editor of three journals: *Groupwork* (Whiting & Birch Publishers), the *Journal of Social Work Practice* (Taylor & Francis), and the *Irish Social Worker* (Irish Association of Social Workers).

Catherine O'Reilly is a Ph.D research student in the School of Education, Trinity College Dublin. A former preschool educator with over 15 years experience, Catherine enrolled at Trinity in 2020 after being awarded a three-year Irish Research Council Postgraduate Scholarship. Her research is devoted to early childhood teaching and learning, with a focus on designing a pedagogical program to draw out emergent critical thinking skills in preschool children through the medium of storytelling.

Carol-Ann O'Síoráin is Assistant Professor of Early Childhood Education in the School of Language, Literacy and Early Childhood in the Institute of Education, Dublin City University (DCU) in Ireland. Carol-Ann is a professional teacher educator with a particular interest in inclusive pedagogical approaches and has been involved in professional teacher education in a number of higher education institutions in Ireland.

Ke Ren (Rita)'s Ph.D research focused on father/dad involvement in early intervention and childhood in Trinity College Dublin, Ireland. Rita is currently a part-time lecturer at St. Nicholas Montessori College, Ireland. Rita's background and continued work as an Early Intervention Specialist concentrates on supporting families of young children with complex needs, particularly those who are from linguistically and culturally diverse background. Her passion to create positive change informs her research agenda, motivating her to develop evidence-based practices to help young children and their families.

Emma Whewell is Associate Professor in Teaching and Learning. She works in the Faculty for Arts, Science and Technology at the University of Northampton, United Kingdom. She is Deputy Subject Leader for Sport and Exercise and the Programme Leader of the B.A. (Hons) Physical Education and Sport degree. She is Co-Lead for the Centre for Active Digital Education at the University of Northampton. She completed her PhD on the formation of identity in newly qualified teachers and her current research focuses upon teaching and learning in higher education, digital pedagogies, mentoring and identity development in teachers.

Preface

There is greater need for a contemporary exploration on not just the practice but the theory of Universal Design for Learning (UDL) and how it drives new applications. There is a greater demand also for application across all aspects of higher education – inside and outside our lecture halls and classrooms. To appreciate the application of UDL, the theory needs to be re-examined in the context of all facets of the higher education system of learning. While there are some excellent practical "how-to" books with respect to UDL, it is more important than ever before that everyone involved in academic teaching and research have a greater understanding of not just what it is and what it means for us, but why and how we can each adopt the philosophy.

The great move to online education and research during Covid-19 highlighted this particular aspect as different faculties and researchers grappled with change and new ways of reaching learners and engaging with their research. The UDL concept would prove to be more useful than ever before, in that it could be applied in so many ways other than had been previously considered. Moreover, while inclusion was only for particular groups prior to this time, as everything moved to a new way of working the inclusion agenda "shifted" and if any academic wanted to remain part the new way of working, they had to work on being included as well as seeking to include.

The book will have a broad appeal and is essentially for anyone looking to implement UDL across learning environments, that is, universities and any education institution. This is a book that can be built on in the future, but it is the foundation of theories that are evolving rapidly with a growing focus on inclusion in teaching, learning and researching. It is targeted at all sectors of the higher education learning environment as they seek to act as a new community, each with a different role to play in ensuring that teaching, learning, and research can be adopted in today's new world.

Preamble

The Power of U

From the outset of this book we wanted to share the "attitude" necessary to promote UDL and inclusion across higher education. To this end we aimed to address some of the most common questions we all engage with on a day-to-day basis as a new way of thinking is emerging:

Is UDL an actual theory or just a new practice?
Is it a bit of a fad?
Isn't it unproved and unscientific?
How is it relevant to my work?
Aren't I doing it anyhow?

We hope we have answered these and so many other questions. But, moreover, we do want to say that the conversation regarding inclusion in education is changing. And as we listen and engage we need to be most aware of our own position and our bias, and moreover we need to join the conversation.

An additional principle for UD or UDL would be **the Power of U** – What you know, have experienced and appreciate in relation to inclusive practice in education; what frames your attitude.

Furthermore, we introduce you to our colleagues who have contributed to this book – the common space being their power and belief in relation to inclusion on campus – their attitude.

DOI: 10.4324/9781003137672-1

Chapter 1

The World before Universal Design (UD) and Universal Design for Learning (UDL)

This book will consider different applications of UDL theory across the higher education campus and will encourage everyone in higher education to consider how UDL can be relevant to their work, whether in the classroom or not. We will take, you, the reader on a journey from the origins of the inclusion agenda – the disability models – through the development of the model of UDL as an innovative way of thinking about inclusion and finally the evolution of this theory in practice that can continue to take into account the new and changing perspectives of inclusion across higher education. This book will include contributions from colleagues, case examples and discussion questions, all supported and reflective of the international research to allow you "to think and see through a UDL lens". The goal is that you (yes you!) will ultimately appreciate your part in supporting the great diversity of learners and colleagues that we meet through our work.

The Changing Face of Higher Education

As the global economy has become more knowledge focused, the opportunity to gain a higher education qualification has become increasingly important. Year on year, our higher education institutions welcome increasing numbers of learners. With this, we also see an increasing diversity among the personal and social characteristics of these learners. Learners from previously under-represented groups are becoming more prevalent. Because this diversity in the learner population will continue to increase, we need to continually develop our institutions, courses, and associated services so as to ensure that all learners feel included. Importantly, these developments are not only visible in relation to our learners. The diversity among those who work in higher education is similarly changing. For everyone in the higher education community, we need to keep evolving – not just to keep pace with these changes – but to demonstrate to wider society that higher education represents the most advanced and ambitious view of what education is – and who can participate in it.

DOI: 10.4324/9781003137672-2

There has been a global increase in the collective awareness about issues related to human rights, learning difficulties, and the need to make education truly inclusive. Educational and social inclusion has the aim of removing obstacles to learning, facilitating participation, and eliminating philosophical and structural barriers. The Covid-19 pandemic was dramatic on many levels and demanded immediate change. It demanded that everyone involved in higher education develop a more nuanced understanding of "active inclusion" – enabling every individual, especially those with real or perceived disadvantage, to fully participate in education and society. As well as our learners, we have all had to seek new ways to feel included – as well as to include – if we wish to work effectively and remain engaged as a community. This represents another key development in the "inclusion agenda". Inclusion has transformed from being "somebody else's business" to being "everyone's business" (McCarthy, Quirke, & Mc Guckin, 2019).

Higher education is one place where we should expect that diversity and individual uniqueness is not simply tolerated, but understood, accepted, and respected (Arduini, 2020). Higher education should have the aim of enhancing our collective understanding of these diversities and individual differences and, from an inclusive perspective, of taking all learners into consideration, emphasising fairness in relation to the nature of their educational needs. Our learner cohorts are not homogenous and there is no such thing as the "average learner". Rather, as the Center for Applied Special Technology (CAST, 2011) reminds us: "In learning environments, such as schools or universities, individual variability is the norm, not the exception" (p. 4).

Before we can begin any proper journey towards the philosophy, principles, and practice of Universal Design (UD) and Universal Design for Learning (UDL), this chapter will set the scene by providing a review of one of the major developments witnessed across the higher education in recent years. A significant change took place when participation from individuals and groups, previously under-represented in our institutions and courses was encouraged by way of policy and access initiatives.

From a historical perspective, many of the major advances in this area have been made in relation to disability and the development of societal thinking about disability. The long-ingrained perspective of society was that a disability or impairment represented something within the person – something that was wrong with them – and something that had to, therefore, be fixed. The hallmarks of this deficit-based "medical model" were dependence and exclusion, and more often thought to mean "less-ability". This perspective has since been largely replaced by the influence of Mike Oliver and others who have advocated for a more "social model" of disability. This perspective is viewed as a more equitable and socially just approach, and has been advocated for strongly by people with disabilities themselves, resulting in the focus shifting from the person to the barriers created by society with an appreciation of how these can "dis-able" an individual. These historical developments have paved the way for thinking about "designing for inclusion" – promoting inclusion by asking people to consider their design approaches from the very beginning.

From an understanding of this historical development in relation to disability, we can reflect upon the increasing diversity of the learners that participate in our higher education institutions and courses. Indeed, it pushes us to ask ourselves, are there still individuals or groups of individuals that are not enabled to profit from the wonderful educational and personal opportunities that we strive to present? Further, would these individuals be enabled to participate if our work represented good practice in terms of UD and UDL principles?

As we have argued, active inclusion in education and society is everyone's business. It is difficult to envisage a role for either UD or UDL in our work if we are unable to reflect on our current practices and be open to changing our own attitudes. At this point, we would ask you to consider this: if we expect the world around us to keep developing and changing, then why should we not expect that we also need to grow, develop, and change? As reflexive practitioners in our work in higher education, our attitudes and behaviours represent what we call "inclusion as process" (Quirke, Mc Guckin, & McCarthy, 2022) – the acknowledgement that the road to inclusion is a journey and not a destination.

The Medical Model of Disability

The definitions and models of disability that have been used by society have been a looking glass that has reflected how disability and people with disabilities have been perceived and treated. Until relatively recently, disability was considered purely in medical terms, whereby a disability was represented as an illness and the person as being dependent. This medical model of disability was dominant and was particularly powerful because different disciplines developed and advocated for this perspective. It could be argued that the medical model resulted in "exclusion" and "segregation" from many parts of society, including education and employment.

A central problem with such medical definitions is that they individualise the "problem" of disability and can transform the description of a condition into a description of a person (McCarthy, 2013). Further, the medical model views all people with a disability as a homogeneous group and excludes all societal factors in relation to disability. This view of disability has also resulted in people with disabilities being "othered" or seen as "negatively different", rather than as being a part of the obvious diversity that exists within the society in which they live. Oliver (1990) recognised that such definitions both medicalise and individualise the problems of disability, as well as the solutions that are put in place. Services for people with disabilities have generally been based upon an individualised and medicalised view of disability – designed by able-bodied people through a process over which disabled people have had little or no control. The outcome has been services and approaches that have been aimed at the individual level, where the emphasis has been upon altering the individual rather than the wider social process (Shakespeare & Watson, 1998).

We are not denying that the medical model of disability can serve a purpose in particular instances – what we are identifying is that it is not the *only* lens through which we can view disability. Whilst it may have served a purpose at a particular time in history, we recognise that disability is not an individual problem to be fixed so that those categorised as "disabled" can lead a "normal" life. In the next section, we consider an alternative view of disability – that postulated through the social model of disability.

The Social Model of Disability

The emergence of the social model of disability in the 1970s was based on a negation of the medical model (Thomas, 2004). This model was advanced by people with disabilities – predominantly those with physical disabilities. It should be noted that there are, in effect, two social models of disability – one originating from the UK with a materialist focus on oppression and the other originating from the US with a minority group focus. The remainder of this section will primarily focus on the UK view of the social model of disability. This model emerged in the late 1970s and is strongly associated with the Union of the Physically Impaired Against Segregation (UPIAS) and Mike Oliver.

Advocates of the social model argue that the medical model over-emphasised the focus on impairment, cure, and rehabilitation. In contrast, the social model asserts that disability is an artificial creation of society and that it (disability) would "vanish almost over-night if social organisation and social attitudes were transformed" (Borsay, 2006, p. 154). Thus, the social model is concerned with the societal barriers that are placed on disabled people (Söder, 2009). At the core of this model is an appreciation that disability should not to be perceived as a personal problem or attribute. Rather, disability should be understood as a complex collection of conditions, many of which are created by the social environment and that "it is society's collective responsibility to make the environmental modifications necessary for the full participation of people with disabilities in all areas of social life" (Duggan & Byrne, 2013, p. 10). The net result of such an approach would see people with disabilities experiencing a better quality of life and more equality of opportunity (Goodley & Tregaskis, 2006).

An obvious criticism of the social model is that it obscures or excludes the realities of impairment (Priestley, 1998). Crow (1996) reminds us that impairment is often an ongoing fact of life for many people with disabilities and therefore cannot be completely omitted from any model of disability that is proposed. While criticisms exist regarding the social model of disability, it must be recognised that the shift towards a social model of disability was the start of a rights-based approach to education (Barton, 1996, 2002) and participation in society.

Evolving Perspectives of Disability

As stated earlier, the medical model and the later social model of disability were the prominent lenses through which disability was viewed within society. Increasingly, there has been a realisation that the way in which we consider disability needs to change, and consequently, in recent decades we have seen the emergence of a number of differing models of disability. These models include the capability approach model, the affirmation model, the cultural model, and the more recent human rights model of disability.

There is an ongoing debate regarding whether models of disabilities are theories. It can be recognised that "[t]heories are often designed from within particular perspectives conceived at particular times in history which do not reflect 'disability' or 'society' as we understand it today" (Corker, 2006, p. 109). Therefore, the emergence of new models of disability may be seen as reflecting the changing ways in which disability is viewed within society.

In recent decades there has been an increased appreciation that individuals with disabilities have historically been excluded from all aspects of society, including political, social, and economic activities. This is reflected in the contemporary view of disability – the human rights model. This model has taken on added significance with the emergence of the Convention on the Rights of Persons with Disabilities (CRPD). The human rights model of disability presents an opportunity to implement the CRPD, with its focus on the inherent dignity of people with disabilities (Degener, 2016). This model of disability is comprehensive, as it encompasses civil, political, economic, social, and cultural rights, which recognise all the realms within which individuals with disabilities can be excluded from society. Importantly, this model also recognises the intersections of disability with, for example, gender, sexuality, and other categories.

As the human rights model of disability becomes more prominent, it is apparent that adopting inclusive practices in every aspect of higher education takes on added significance. These changes also align with the philosophy and practice that underlies UD and UDL, ensuring that inclusion is actively embedded within everything we do.

The human rights–based view recognises that individuals with disabilities are experts in their own lives and, consequently, need to be recognised as vital in decisions about all aspects of their lives. Our focus here is not to present a detailed analysis of the "inclusion agenda" within primary and post-primary education. Suffice to say, various international agreements and national legislative instruments have witnessed a large and sustained inclusion of pupils in schools who would previously have been excluded from the opportunity of getting access to an education in their local school with their non-disabled peers. When we see the success of these inclusion approaches and reasonable accommodations, it is understandable that we are seeing a greater number of the pupils now seeking access to further education and training (FET), and to higher education.

In Ireland, recent policy and practice initiatives in the FET sector have seen UD and UDL becoming front and centre of active inclusion at a national level (see Heelan & Tobin, 2021; Quirke & McCarthy, 2020). We argue that the onus is on each and every one of us involved in higher education to take the initiative – in our separate disciplines and service areas – to reflect upon current practices and assumptions – and explore how and where a UD and UDL approach might make our campuses accessible for the greatest number of learners from the "get-go" (Quirke, McCarthy, Treanor, & Mc Guckin, 2019).

An Evolving Appreciation of Learning and Inclusion

Working in a learning environment, we are very privileged to be part of our learners' development, watching them think, learn, grow, and develop – educationally, emotionally, and psychologically. The thinking of key development and lifespan psychologists present us with understandings about how our learners grow and develop. In this section of the chapter, we briefly indicate some of the key thinkers, and how a basic understanding of their work can be beneficial to our practice in higher education and activities related to active inclusion.

Important in the context of education is the work of Jean Piaget and those who developed his early work (e.g., Margaret Donaldson). Piaget and his followers helped us to understand how we develop our thinking and cognition across various developmental stages, with each of us being capable of increasing complexity in cognition as we grow from babies through childhood into early adolescence and adulthood. Piaget always reminds us that babies and children act as "little scientists" in their environment, learning through trial and error, using their natural instincts to learn about the world around them. In our work in higher education, we also seek to encourage our learners to act similarly. This is one of the hallmarks of UDL theory and practice.

From a more social perspective, Erik Erikson gave us a very good understanding as to how we develop "psycho-socially" –that is, how the people around us help us to develop a sense of who we are. An important concept that Erikson draws our intention to is the issue of identity. For example, we have all survived adolescence, a key stage in psychosocial development whereby each of us had to unconsciously start to develop a sense of who we are, distinct from our parents and peers. We could argue that each of our learners, regardless of age or stage of development, is continuing on their journey of exploring their identity. As we reflect on each of these theories, we can identify that learning, transitioning, and social engagement are key factors in developing inclusive approaches in higher education.

The work of the Behaviourists in the early part of the 20th century (e.g., Watson, Skinner, Thorndike) also helped us to understand learning as a series of "stimulus–response" events. For example, when we are teaching our new puppy to "sit!", we can see that the more often we pair a treat with the command to sit, the puppy gradually learns that there is a relationship between you asking it to sit and getting that treat! That is, the stimulus is the treat and the response is the behaviour. Can you think of instances where we reward inclusive practices and behaviours, and how these enable such positive behaviours to develop more?

Extending this work, we can see the great benefit of Bandura's social learning theory, and how we learn by "imitation" and "modelling". We learn from watching what others are doing – modelling what we see. Vygotsky's notions of "scaffolding" and the "zone of proximal development" similarly help us to understand how learners can "reach" beyond what they might be capable of when their learning is scaffolded and when we support them in their trials and errors. UDL builds its thinking on such theories.

Newer thinking about intelligence from Dweck helps us to understand the difference between having a "fixed mindset" and a "growth mindset" – whether we play safe and do not take risks for fear of getting the problem wrong or whether we see errors as opportunities to learn. Dweck helpfully posits that we have "the power of yet" – the idea that whilst I got the answer incorrect this time, it is just that I do not know the answer or mechanics of how to resolve the problem "yet"! With so much of social and learning interaction now being conducted online, we see the importance of Bowlby's attachment theory (and the subsequent work of Mary Ainsworth and Mary Main) in educational settings – that is, that the quality, strength, and consistency of attachments and relationships with others has importance for the healthy psychological and learning development of the individual. For example, are our attachments to the academic environment warm, stable, and consistent? Or are they cold, detached, and not predictable?

Urie Bronfenbrenner presents us with a really important understanding of how the developing individual cannot be divorced from the people and environment around them. In his "ecological" theory, Bronfenbrenner demonstrates that we have important bi-directional and influential relationships with people and events at home, at college, and the wider world. In putting the "person in context", Bronfenbrenner helps us to understand the "individual in context" – helping us to understand that these different parts of development do not happen in isolation from our college life, family life, participation in clubs and societies on campus, and wider social participation, and moreover the important role that the wider world plays in terms of individual learning experience and the wider aspect of policies, laws, and global issues, and aspirations. And so context is everything.

The combined understanding that we can get from each of these small reviews enables us to start developing a more holistic perspective as to how we develop and learn, but moreover – how we need to appreciate and develop an attitude for inclusion. Attitude is of the essence!

From Exclusion to Inclusion

For some of us, we might have had more experience with feelings and experiences of being excluded, rather than any great memories or good examples of being made to feel included. Throughout our time in education, from our first days at primary school right through to now, we might have had the experience of being excluded from games or sporting activities, birthday parties, or even more seriously, being bullied.

The common discourse in education and society focuses predominantly on issues related to inclusion and everyone's wish to feel understood and included, recognised for their own uniqueness, and to be treated on an equal basis with everyone else. Less attention is directed to conversations and action related to policies, practices, and individual behaviours that are exclusionary – either deliberately and with malevolent intent or inadvertent but nonetheless hurtful in the resultant experience.

From this reflection, and as part of our own individual journeys towards the development and application of UD and UDL principles in our work, we need to remember that focusing on active inclusion is only one part of the task. The other part is to consider where there might be blind spots in either our own individual practices or those of the institution or department that we work in. In doing this reflexive work, we might need to solicit, in an open and encouraging way, the views and opinions of those towards whom our work is directed – and these are, for the most part, our learners.

What Does This Journey Look Like as a "Lived Experience"?

It is evident that there have been many positive social and educational changes over recent decades. This chapter has highlighted the changes that have occurred in relation to the some of the more prominent models of disabilities, and how these have had a positive impact on the lives of people with disabilities. As mentioned, from an "inclusion as process" perspective, our work in this area is a journey rather than a destination.

In our task of reviewing the development of thinking and practice in education and society – from the deficit-based medical model of disability to the more inclusive social model of disability – and indeed the more contemporary approaches (e.g., social justice), it is useful to take time to reflect upon two separate personal narratives from individuals who have succeeded in higher education. These narratives exemplify the issues that have been reviewed in the chapter. Both narratives could be viewed as examples of individual tenacity and determination – and worthy of our congratulations and admiration.

In the first narrative, Dr Patricia McCarthy (one of the authors of this book) recounts her journey of personal determination to access the same right to education and participation in society that was afforded naturally to her non-disabled siblings. Patricia clearly identifies as being "a disabled person" – rather than using "person-first" terminology (i.e., being a person first and the disability being secondary to this). Patricia's story of her personal and educational journey is informative for us as it clearly sets out how access and participation in education and society were not seen as natural.

From a different perspective regarding educational inclusion, Dr Cristina Devecchi's (University of Northampton) personal narrative extends Patricia's story, in that, whilst it is not set against a backdrop of disability, it is an example of exclusionary thinking and practice. Cristina's story helps us to understand that the same underlying themes of prejudicial thought and discriminatory actions were evident, even for non-disabled individuals.

Both of the personal narratives are about inclusion – albeit as both Patricia and Cristina experienced exclusion. All too often we hear comments that successful individuals like Patricia and Cristina are "inspirational" in that they challenged and overcame the adversities that confronted them. However, we really need to see these as historical examples, and as the exception to the norm, whereby we advocate for a higher education system where the atypical is the typical. Not only do we need to think this way in terms of the diversity of learners that we meet on our higher education campuses, but we need to see this diversity among our colleagues also.

Dr Patricia McCarthy

Here, one of the authors of this book, Dr Patricia McCarthy, presents a personal reflection on how the models of disability have had an influence on her life.

Beginning school in Ireland in the 1970s as a vision-impaired child meant that there was very little choice, except to attend a special "school for the blind". For many, including me, this was not a choice. It was the norm for children who were diagnosed with a significant vision impairment or who were blind. This was not just the norm in Ireland – it was like this across most of the world. Why was this? Well, it was primarily influenced by the model of disability that was prominent at the time – that is, a medical model of disability which identified me and others like me by our diagnosis. It was believed that blind and vision-impaired children had significantly greater educational needs than their peers and, therefore, needed to be educated in segregated institutionalised settings.

The consequence of this medical model thinking and its influence on educational policy meant that I had to leave my home and family, and move over 250 kilometres away to a "special school", where I boarded and was able to return home only three times each year. Whilst 250 kilometres may not sound like a huge distance to travel today, we need to remember that this was at a time when the road and transport network was quite under-developed in Ireland, and that private car ownership was not typical. This was a difficult decision for my mother. However, she believed that I deserved an education just like my siblings had received, and that this was the only real option available to me as a vision-impaired child.

All children in the school were either vision impaired or blind, and many of us used Braille as our primary means of learning. There was no option for me to attend a mainstream school in my own locality at the time, as teachers did not have the knowledge or experience required to teach somebody with a significant vision impairment – or indeed many of the issues that were subsequently called "special educational needs". Therefore, it was very unusual for children with a range of disabilities to be educated alongside their non-disabled peers in their local school. The result of this was that disability was often not visible within local communities, and this subsequently perpetuated the negative notions around disability and disabled people.

I was amongst the first cohort of pupils in the school I attended to participate in the state examinations. This was largely due to our parents, including my own mother, advocating to enable us to have the right, like our non-disabled peers, to have this opportunity. However, there was little or no expectation that I would transition to higher education, even though I had a desire and capability to do so. Again, this was influenced by the medical model of disability that was prominent in Ireland at the time. This model of disability did not recognise my ability. Rather, it created a focus on impairment and, therefore, labelled me "different".

When I left post-primary education, again my choices were limited. Particular areas of study, such as computer programming, were deemed appropriate for me. Why? Mainly because I was vision impaired. There was no recognition of my abilities or what I might want or like to do. Rather, it was others – namely "professionals" – who knew best and what was appropriate for me at the time. This demonstrates how the policies and practices that were underpinned by the medical model of disability impacted on my own life and those of other disabled people.

Changes in society can influence the life trajectory of disabled people. In the second half of the 1990s there was a notable shift away from the medical model perspective to a more social model perspective. In the late 1990s I took the opportunity to enter higher education. This was influenced by many things, including the fact that there was a shift in attitude around what disabled people could do, what they wanted to do, and what they might like to do. There was also a national policy change that saw the introduction of free fees for study at higher education. And so I returned to mainstream education in 1997. My experience here was very different from that of my time in special school, due in part to the fact that societal attitudes towards disabled people were beginning to change and there were the beginnings of a concerted effort to ensure that more disabled learners were given the opportunity to enter higher education. Policies were implemented that meant that supports were now available within higher education institutions to provide the necessary accommodations for disabled learners. These enabled me to participate on an equal level with my non-disabled peers. This illustrates how changes in society at the levels of policy and practice can have a direct impact on the lives of disabled people.

It is important to recognise that changes in society regarding how disability and disabled people are viewed are influenced in large, by whichever is the dominant model of disability. Consequently, I am hoping that the rights-based approach, which is taking on added significance as a result of the United Nations Convention on the Rights of Persons with Disabilities (UNCRPD), will ensure that disabled people (including myself) will soon have the same opportunities as everyone else in society. This is where UD and UDL are significant, as they ensure that environments (including learning) can – to the greatest extent possible – be inclusive of everyone. So, while many people think of the models of disability only in a theoretical context, it is important that we consider how these models impact the lives of people like me. This is why I keep reiterating that "inclusion is everyone's business".

Patricia's story helps us to understand some of the central issues that are related to social justice and participation in education and society. Whilst Patricia's story is a classic example of how a disabled person's educational and life choices were given direction by the prevailing social thinking about disability, the following personal story extends this discussion by demonstrating that exclusion and barriers to education have also existed for many people who are not disabled.

Our very good colleague Professor Cristina Devecchi (University of Northampton) recounts her personal experience of the barriers that she encountered in her educational journey – from being a child in Italy, to her current research and applied practice in the UK as a specialist in issues related to special educational needs/disability, and inclusion in education and society.

Professor Cristina Devecchi

Fifty Years of Inclusion: What Next?

History is the collage of stories, events, and happenings that, in shaping and reshaping the present, open up possibilities for imagining possible futures. It is with this view of "a life lived" that I introduce how my early childhood educational and social experiences have shaped my understanding and practice of disability and inclusion. In essence, these have – one layer at a time – built my "being inclusive".

I was born at the tail-end of the boom generation, in a small town in the North-West of the industrial triangle, in Italy. I remember, vaguely, watching the historical moon landing on a black-and-white television set, the rotary-dial telephone stuck to a wall, and many other "historical" objects which more recent generations regard as nostalgic collectable antiques. Undoubtedly, many things have changed since then, mostly in technological leaps and bounds, which have opened up the world to us, democratised knowledge, connected us to the world and brought that world into our homes and minds in real time, all the time. Technologies which have also restricted our world to what we like, reducing us to a form of technological labour, slaves to algorithms which entice us with personalisation and rob us of our person and being.

In my account I take a broad definition of inclusion as pertaining to the moral, legal, and practical aspects of removing barriers to access, participation, and achievement. I do contend that individuals are excluded – based on many of their characteristics – some physical, some cognitive, some economic, or based on their religious or ethnic background. In most cases, it is the combination of one or more of these characteristics that "dis-ables" the individual by boxing them into stereotypes of ability, thus carving out boundaries between the deserving and underserving, building walls of incomprehension, misunderstandings, and failure.

I vividly remember issues with difference and discrimination while in primary school. My classmates, all girls, included the children of professional parents from the North and the blue-collar workers from the South. Within the four walls of my classroom we were told we were all equal, all Italian, all together. But, when the bell rang and we walked out of the school, I remember seeing the mothers waiting outside: the ones from the North on one side, and the ones from the South, mainly wearing traditional black dresses, on the other. By the time I stepped out of the school gate, two "Italy-ies" walked in different directions.

It did not take me long to understand that there were more ways of carving out differences amongst us. In 1975, I transferred to lower secondary school. I chose the closest school to my home because I wanted to study German and that was the only school in the area that was teaching German at the time. Little did I know, but that to cope with the closure of "differential classes" (i.e., classes for those pupils who required specialised attention), the school had decided to move all of those children from the differential classes into the German classes – the perception being that these children needed an environment that was strict and disciplined. My father was called in and the headteacher explained that his daughter would have been better in Section A or B (i.e., Class A or B), where there were other children like her. That is, whose parents were from a professional background and whose children were academically more gifted. I must give credit to my father. He replied that it was my decision which language to learn and that, in any case, children should all study together irrespective of who their parents were.

I spent three valuable years working as a teaching assistant, helping young men who had repeated so many of their school years (i.e., not permitted to advance through the school years until they attained certain levels of attainment), that they were now very close to their age for military service. My education did not suffer. On the contrary, I learned from my teachers the importance of supporting everybody. I also learned German.

I did not realise the importance of those early formative experiences until I applied 30-odd years later for a job as a Learning Support Assistant (LSA) in a secondary school in the UK. There my role was to support children with disabilities and/or Special Educational Needs (SEN). Or, as a colleague of mine said, provide TLC, (tender loving care), because "you can take a horse to water, but you can't make it drink". Implied in her view was that "some" children could not fit in, could not achieve, and the only thing that we could do was to alleviate the pain of failure. Needless to say, I disagreed. Not only that, I could also see that the "deficit" model was so pervasive that it also impacted on how teachers viewed LSAs and the SENCO (Special Educational Needs Co-ordinator). So I enrolled in a Master's in Special and Inclusive Education at the University of Cambridge, but soon realised that you cannot be an LSA if you have a Master's and the teachers you support don't have one! I found myself excluded and decided to continue my studies and gain a PhD.

The Master's and PhD years added theory to what I had learnt through my experience and practice as an LSA and as a teacher of Italian in Lebanon where we went for a few years. They also opened up my understanding of different models of disability and theories of inclusion, equality, and social justice. They allowed me to go deeper into educational theory, but also to learn from other disciplines, such as philosophy, sociology, and economics. Those years also showed me that even in a highly academic environment, discrimination and exclusion happen. I am now teaching in a university and realise that the struggle to be inclusive is never-ending, relentlessly asking you to be alert to what is evidently exclusion, and what lurks imperceptibly in everyday small gestures, attitudes, and ways of working. The point I want to make is that there was no golden age of "full inclusion". Rather, each generation has had to deal with specific challenges to inclusion.

I want to conclude this account of 50 years of being inclusive with a positive outlook. There are rays of hope which hint at a change of perspective on what really matters for a life worth living. Concerns about climate change, post-pandemic rebuilding, mental and physical health, to mention just a few, have highlighted the fact that economic growth, per se, is not enough to build a fair and just world. Whilst inclusion was born out of a humanitarian concern for human rights, I suggest to add to this a more humanistic approach to building a world which is fit for everybody. While the models we have developed to understand human frailty are useful, they are useless if we do not change our moral perspective on what it means to be a person. For this reason, I call for a shift toward a humane approach, one which starts from the intrinsic value of each and every human being, and while acknowledging our limitations, be them physical, psychological, or economic, it allows us to keep hope and surprise in what we can achieve together.

Conclusion

Many people working in higher education can identify with the exclusionary practices and experiences recounted by Patricia and Cristina. Through widening participation initiatives over recent times, many colleagues have been able to access and participate in higher education courses. Not only that, many have been able to make the transition from being a higher education learner to being part of the higher education working community.

Both stories help us to recognise that as time progresses, we increasingly appreciate that higher education needs to become more open, equitable, and accessible to the diversity of learners who would like the opportunity to participate in our courses. The time is now to acknowledge that we need to begin designing our institutions, campuses, courses, and learner experiences to be accessible and encouraging from the "get-go" – that is, now is the opportune time to develop our thinking and practice in terms of UD and UDL.

Points to Consider

Having read this chapter:

- How are the concepts discussed in this chapter relevant within your higher education institution today?
- What do you think might personally challenge you in working towards "Inclusion", "Universal Design" and "Universal Design for Learning"?
- What current social issues do we need to consider when we think about inclusion?
- What do you already know about active inclusion on your campus and what do you think would be an easy win for you, your colleagues, and your learners?

- There can be many "moving parts" when considering UDL and inclusion for higher education. Having read this chapter, and reflected on the content and case examples – we now ask – how might this shape your attitude to UD and UDL higher education?

References

Arduini, G. (2020). Curriculum innovation with universal design for learning. *Education Sciences & Society – Open Access*, *11*(1), 90–103. Retrieved from: https://ojs.francoangeli.it/_ojs/index.php/ess/article/view/9460 https://doi.org/10.3280/ess1-2020oa9460

Barton, L. (1996). Sociology and disability: some emerging issues. In L. Barton (Ed.), *Disability and society: Emerging issues and insights* (pp. 3–17). London: Longman.

Barton, L. (2002). Inclusive education and the management of change in Britain. *Exceptionality Education Canada*, *12*(2–3), 169–185.

Borsay, A. (2006). Personal trouble or public issue? Towards a model of policy for people with physical and mental disabilities. In L. Barton (Ed.), *Overcoming disabling barriers: 18 years of disability & society* (pp. 161–178). London: Routledge.

Center for Applied Special Technology. (CAST). (2011). *Universal design for learning (UDL) guidelines: Full-text representation. Version 2.0.* Wakefield, MA.

Corker, M. (2006). Differences, conflations and foundations: The limits to 'accurate' theoretical representation of disabled people's experiences? In L. Barton (Ed.), *Overcoming disabling barriers: 18 years of disability & society* (pp. 108–124). London: Taylor & Francis.

Crow, L. (1996). Including all of our lives: Renewing the social model of disability. In J. Morris (Ed.), *Encounters with strangers: Feminism and disability* (pp. 206–226). London: Women's Press.

Degener, T. (2016). A human rights model of disability. In P. Blanck & E. Flynn (Eds.), *Routledge handbook of disability law and human rights* (pp. 47–66). London: Routledge.

Duggan, C., & Byrne, M. (2013). *What works in the provision of higher, further and continuing education, training and rehabilitation for adults with disabilities. A Review of the literature.* Trim, Ireland: National Council for Special Education.

Goodley, D., & Tregaskis, C. (2006). Storying disability and impairment: Retrospective accounts of disabled family life. *Qualitative Health Research*, *16*(5), 630–646. https://doi.org/10.1177/1049732305285840

Heelan, A., & Tobin, T. (2021). *UDL for FET practitioners. Guidance for implementing universal design for learning in Irish further education and training.* Dublin, IE: SOLAS & AHEAD Ireland. Retrieved from: https://www.solas.ie/f/70398/x/81044b80ce/fet_practitioners-main.pdf

McCarthy, P. (2013). *Expectations you encounter: The educational experiences and transition choices/opportunities of blind/vision impaired people in the Republic of Ireland.* [Unpublished PhD thesis]. Trinity College Dublin, Ireland.

McCarthy, P., Quirke, M., & Mc Guckin, C. (2019). UDL – Can you see what I see … is it an exclusive model or an inclusive model? *Third Pan-Canadian Conference* on *Universal Design for Learning: Connecting the Dots – Sharing Promising Practices across Country*, 2nd–4th October, 2019, Royal Roads University, Victoria, Canada. Abstracts not published.

Oliver, M. (1990). *The politics of disablement: A sociological approach*. London: Macmillan Education.

Priestley, M. (1998). Constructions and creations: Idealism, materialism and disability theory. *Disability & Society*, *13*(1), 75–94. https://doi.org/10.1080/09687599826920

Quirke, M., Mc Guckin, C., & McCarthy, P. (2022). How to adopt an "inclusion as process" approach and navigate ethical challenges in research. In *SAGE research methods cases*. London, United Kingdom: SAGE Publications, Ltd. https://doi.org/10.4135/9781529605341

Quirke, M., & McCarthy, P. (2020). *A conceptual framework of universal design for learning (UDL) for the Irish further education and training sector: Where inclusion is everybody's business*. Dublin, IE: SOLAS & AHEAD Ireland. Retrieved from: https://www.solas.ie/f/70398/x/b1aa8a51b6/a-conceptual-framework-of-universal-design-for-learning-udl-for-the-ir.pdf

Quirke, M., McCarthy, P., Treanor, D., & Mc Guckin, C. (2019). Tomorrow's disability officer – A cornerstone on the universal design campus. *Journal of Inclusive Practice in Further and Higher Education (JIPFHE)*, *11*(1), 29–42.

Shakespeare, T., & Watson, N. (1998). Theoretical perspectives on research with disabled children. In C. Robinson & K. Stalker (Eds.), *Growing up with disability: Research highlights in social work* (pp. 13–27). London: Jessica Kingsley.

Söder, M. (2009). Tensions, perspectives and themes in disability studies. *Scandinavian Journal of Disability Research*, *11*(2), 67–81. https://doi.org/10.1080/15017410902830496

Thomas, C. (2004). Disability and impairment. In J. Swain, S. French, C. Barnes, & C. Thomas (Eds.), *Disabling barriers – Enabling environments*. London: SAGE.

Chapter 2

Universal Design

Chapter 1 provided us with an understanding of how our thinking about active inclusion and inclusive education has developed from a very medicalised and deficit-based approach to the understanding of individuals who have a disability towards a more social and human rights perspective that views disability as being largely a by-product of how we organise society. As this social and inclusive approach was developing, with very positive and demonstrable applications in education, so too was a similar advancement in the thinking about how we should design buildings, the wider built environment, products, and services to be inclusive of all individuals (i.e., UD).

Society is not composed of individuals who are perfect. In terms of product design, the most important factor to be considered is the end user – you and me. Designers fully understand that there is no such thing as "the average person" – average in each anthropomorphic dimension. As unique as our fingerprints, we all have different physical dimensions, with different ability levels in relation to motor, visual, auditory, and cognitive functioning. Neither are we static – we are each continually moving through the universally predetermined stages of our lives – from the clunky and clumsy early stages of toddlerhood and the play years, through the rapid biological and social developments of adolescence, and onwards through early and middle adulthood towards a slowing down of development in later adulthood. In terms of the focus of Chapter 1, each one of us will experience either a temporary or permanent disability at some point in our life.

Before we can consider how we might advocate for a UD attitude and approach to learning and experience in higher education (e.g., UDL), it is necessary to firstly set out the foundational principles of Universal Design (UD). From its initial development within the field of architecture in the 1980s, UD is an approach that sets about creating inclusive thinking in the designs for buildings, products, and services so that they can be accessed by the greatest number of users possible – from the "get-go" (Story, Mueller, & Mace, 1998). This chapter explores the foundations and central principles of UD and how these have inspired others to develop and apply this thinking to

DOI: 10.4324/9781003137672-3

inclusive education. As you read through this chapter, you might recognise some of these design features, and you might even realise that you have already implemented some of them in your work for the learners that you support in higher education. However, like the rest of us, what you might also recognise is that when you have enacted one or more of these principles already, you have probably done so "by accident rather than by design". Perhaps, read this chapter in a reflexive manner and consider how and where you might be able to adapt or change current practices in your work to be more UD friendly. Moving towards UD practice does not have to happen in one big movement. Rather, as advocated by Behling and Tobin (2018), you could work in a "plus one" manner – identifying just one area of practice where you could create just one more way of doing something that is currently done, adjusting current approaches to be more in line with the philosophy and action of UD. From this incremental perspective, UD becomes easy to embed in ongoing thinking and planning.

Ron Mace and the Development of Universal Design

The term "Universal Design" was first proposed by the architect Ron Mace (North Carolina State University) in 1985. As a wheelchair user, Mace had personal experience of the challenges presented by traditional approaches to building and product design. From these experiences, Mace advocated for an approach that moved away from the "add-on" or "reactionary" thinking around "inclusion" and physical spaces. Mace's concept of UD set out an approach for the design of products and the built environment so that they could be both aesthetic and usable – to the greatest extent possible – regardless of the user's age, ability, or status in life (Jones, 2010; Mace, 2008).

Importantly, UD is not an approach that is to be targeted at any particular group of individuals and it is not influenced by factors such as the economy, education, status, or ability. Rather, it is a comprehensive and straightforward approach to design that can truly realise the equality of all people. In many instances, the application of UD thinking may only require slight modifications to things, such as the size, shape, or even the placement of an item. Mace's team of architects, designers, engineers, and researchers at the Center for Universal Design at North Carolina State University set out their definition of UD as: "Universal design is the design of products and environments to be usable by all people, to the greatest extent possible, without adaptation or specialized design" (Connell et al., 1997).

Thus, UD provides a framework of recommended accommodation guidelines for architects, builders, and interior designers to consider as they navigate the creative process towards a widely usable environment or product. Put simply, UD refers to the design of the built environment, products, and services so that they can be used by the greatest number of people without the need for special design or adjustment – starting from the concept that it is more convenient to design buildings and objects with prior consideration of the differences that characterise individuals (Zeng & Jiang, 2014). It is important to note here that UD does not promise that there will never be the need for amendments to designs and products. To do so would be arrogant and would ignore the rich diversity that exists among us all. Indeed, Article 2 (Definitions) of the UN Convention on the Rights of Persons with Disabilities (UNCRPD) notes that UD shall not exclude assistive devices for particular groups of persons with disabilities where this is needed. It would be difficult to imagine any design approach that could be fully accessible by each and every one of us. We are all unique in terms of ability and preference for how we engage with the environment around us. UD acknowledges this in terms of the aspiration to design "to the greatest extent possible". It should be relatively easy for each of us to see examples of UD in the design and accessibility of our own institutions and the buildings that we all use. Examples of UD in practice include:

- Ramp entrances;
- Automatic doors;
- Elevators;
- Public toilets with larger stalls;
- Height-accessible service desks;
- Low-floor bus;
- Captioned videos/open-captioned television (e.g., used by most news channels);
- Information/materials provided in multiple forms (e.g., standard, electronic, large print, Braille);
- Accessible websites;
- Remote controls;
- Automatic sanitisation dispensers.

Reasonable Accommodations in Higher Education

For many of us involved in education, we can understand some of the philosophy of UD in terms of the "reasonable accommodations" that may be provided for learners so that they can participate in their studies on an equal basis with their peers. Examples of reasonable accommodations in higher education include adjusting the format of printed materials, providing audio or video recordings of lectures, and providing extra time in examinations. The important thing to remember here is that a reasonable accommodation does not, and should not, confer an advantage to the learner. Rather, the accommodation is a simple amendment to the learning process to provide equitable access and participation. Through our recent experience with Covid-19, we have seen how some of these accommodations that were originally only available to learners with a disability have become very useful to all learners (e.g., recorded lectures, time extensions for examinations).

Reasonable accommodations for learners with a disability are provided because we are legally compelled to do so. However, when we think about this issue in a wider sense, much of what we design and provide for in higher education is predicated on the mythical "average person" and there are rarely differentiated approaches to what we do. There is rarely any recognition of the variety of individual differences that are presented in our learner cohorts. We generally have only one approach to things like recruitment and advertising, registration and registry, library resources and access, lectures, seminars and labs, assessment, and engagement with clubs, societies, and college services.

As higher education becomes busier each year with the increasing numbers of learners that we welcome to our institutions, we can start to appreciate that various reasonable accommodations that have been provided to learners who have disclosed that they have a disability are of great benefit to all learners. With increasing registrations, we also see a greater diversity amongst the non-traditional learners who make up our higher education institutions (e.g., learners from other countries and cultures, learners from widening participation initiatives, mature learners). To be more contemporary in what we do, we are increasingly moving from traditional face-to-face lectures and seminars toward a hybrid or fully online model of participation. With ongoing developments from colleagues with an interest in assistive technology, artificial intelligence, virtual reality, and augmented reality, there will be an increased onus on everyone in higher education to adapt current attitudes and practices to become beneficial to learner expectations and requirements.

The Seven Principles of Universal Design

To guide architects and designers, Mace and colleagues (Story et al., 1998) conceptualised UD in terms of seven guiding principles, each with useful interpretable guidelines. The goal of these principles is to set out the criteria that can guide the design process and ensure that inclusion for individual differences is consciously considered from the outset. As noted above, it is important to recognise that this approach does not seek to negate the need for add-on supports for groups or individuals who might find themselves excluded without them. Therefore, this approach demands a mindful and perhaps more "positive approach" to inclusion. As with many useful frameworks and guiding principles, we would encourage you to see these seven principles as "yardstick rather than templates" for your work. In conjunction with Behling and Tobin's (2018) "plus one" approach, read through each of the seven principles below and consider them in terms of what you are responsible for in terms of our learners in higher education.

When we read the names and initial descriptions of the principles, we need to remember that these were developed for architects and designers. However, in a similar manner, we are also architects and designers – albeit in our various roles within higher education. When reading through the principles, it is worth keeping in mind our roles and how these principles could be easily applied to our planned interactions with the learners that we support.

Principle One: Equitable Use

From a pure UD perspective, Equitable Use means that the design should be useful and marketable to people with a diverse range of abilities (Huff, 2020). In practice, this principle advises us that we should provide the same means of use for all of our learners – "identical whenever possible; equivalent when not" (American Library Association: ALA, 2006). In adhering to this principle, we are ensuring that what we do is appealing to the learners and that we can be confident that our approach will not disadvantage or stigmatise any group of learners. Also, provisions for safety, security, and privacy should be equally available to all users.

For us, this means that our teaching, assessment, and provision of services should be designed "with intent" from the "get-go" to be as inclusive as possible for as many learners as possible – without the need for subsequent add-ons or modifications. As well as their institutional biography web entry, many academics also have personal websites and social media accounts that they use to promote their teaching and research. Whilst we might assume that the official institutional biography page complies with UD and Human Computer Interaction (HCI) standards enacted by the organisation's web developers, a key question arises regarding the personal pages and accounts of academics – do the website or blog posts, for example, facilitate text-to-speech software? Do images also contain "alt-text" for screen reader software to know what the image is and a description of the image's contents for learners who are blind or visually impaired?

Principle Two: Flexibility in Use

Flexibility in Use is all about the provision of choice in methods of use. This means that the design should be able to accommodate a wide range of individual preferences and abilities (Huff, 2020). In practice, this would result in, for example, the provision of a choice in methods for a learner to use, presenting accommodations for right- or left-handed access and use, providing adaptability to the learner's pace, and facilitating the learner's accuracy and precision (ALA, 2006).

In terms of what we are interested in, we need to consider the development of, for example, materials that we might wish to provide. If you need the learner to provide their consent to participate in an event or research project, are you relying solely on a printed form with information and check-boxes? Similarly, if there are instructions or information about your service or programme, are these only available in printed format? To be flexible in use, you might wish to consider alternative presentation and response styles – maybe providing a

YouTube video with the information, perhaps an audio version of the information, or enabling consent to be provided through a recorded voice message.

A useful example of Flexibility in Use is the moving walkway that we often see in airports. Whilst we might prefer to walk to the departure gate, we might also prefer to use the option of the moving walkway. Some of us might walk on this to help speed up our journey, some users may use it if they are tired or have mobility issues. Users who are traveling with young children might use the walkway to reduce fatigue. To reduce my own fatigue whilst redrafting this section of the chapter, when I got jaded typing up my notes and new content, I used the "dictate" function in the word-processing package – again, a useful example of this principle in everyday action for someone in higher education.

Principle Three: Simple and Intuitive Use

Across all of the activities that we expect applicants and learners to engage in, we need to remain cognisant of the need to ensure that what we have designed is simple, intuitive, and easy to understand – regardless of the user's knowledge, language skills, or current concentration level (Huff, 2020).

This always sounds easy. But it isn't! We generally tend to design things in a manner that is pleasing to ourselves individually, or maybe with some inspiration for the fictional "average person" that will use, or engage with, what we have designed. Unless you have some previous skills and education that are specifically related to design principles, it is really difficult to know if you have a design that is both simple and intuitive. Most of us have great ideas for something that is based on sound practical or professional knowledge. However, unless we pilot our work and perhaps use focus groups of end users, our approaches are, at best, naïve and probably destined for failure. Remember – you can have the most technically sophisticated design – but it is useless if the user cannot understand it or navigate their way through it. In terms of designing for simple and intuitive use, we should strive to eliminate unnecessary complexity, be consistent with the expectations and intuition of the applicant or learner, accommodate for a wide range of language and literacy skills, arrange the required information in a manner that is consistent with its importance, and provide effective prompting and feedback during and after task completion (ALA, 2006).

Principle Four: Perceptible Information

At first glance, this principle seems to be much more related to the built environment than anything that most of us might be doing. As a UD principle, Perceptible Information relates to whether the design communicates all of the necessary information effectively to the user, regardless of ambient conditions (e.g., distractions) or the user's sensory abilities (Huff, 2020).

If we translate this to the work that we might be planning, we could imagine this principle in two distinct ways. Firstly, we could interpret it in terms of structural and built environment issues – for example, to what extent does our service or programme need to have access to a sports hall, a particular laboratory, learning space, or event location (e.g., graduation), or to some aspects of nature (e.g., field trip, professional practice placement)? Do you require a particular style of lighting or room layout that is different from normal? Secondly, we could interpret this principle in terms of the materials used for the construction of the intervention or programme. Is there something important to be communicated in the style of the packaging to be used or the materials that the learners will interact with – and does this require a certain level of sensory abilities (e.g., brochure, identification card, formal communication about registration, participation, or results)? Remember that sensory ability is much more than whether the learner has a visual or hearing impairment. Many learners who are autistic or who experience a neuro-developmental challenge prefer certain sensory and tactile experiences over others.

Guidelines based on this principle advise us to use different modes (pictorial, verbal, tactile) for redundant presentation of essential information, maximise the "legibility" of essential information (e.g., use various levels of contrast between essential information and the surrounding information), differentiate elements in ways that can be described (i.e., make it easy to give instructions or directions), and provide compatibility with a variety of techniques or devices used by people with sensory limitations (ALA, 2006). For many of us, we experience this principle in practice when we are on vacation and visit a museum or take a bus tour – information can be provided in tactile, visual, or auditory modes – or perhaps all of these simultaneously. Just as a tour operator or museum might increase foot-fall by being able to advertise that all of these methods of experiencing their services are available, so too would our higher education institutions benefit from increased applications and increases in learner experiences.

Principle Five: Tolerance for Error

Like principle four, Tolerance for Error might seem to be an issue more akin to buildings and the built environment. Tolerance for Error means that the design will seek to minimise hazards and possible adverse consequences of accidental or unintended actions (Huff, 2020).

For our purposes, we probably will not have (hopefully!) any hazards associated with the design and implementation of our services or courses. If, for example, we have designed a computerised or virtual reality (VR) "serious game" scenario (perhaps for recruitment purposes), are there well understood feedback mechanisms for when a user makes unintentional errors? Would the user be safely guided back to the safety of where they should be? If it is a VR intervention or programme, is the immediate physical environment safe? For us, we should interpret the "consequences of accidental or unintended actions" to be not just about physical danger to health and well-being, and also related to consequences related to self-esteem and self-perceptions of ability.

Whilst the guidelines associated with this principle are more directly understood in the planning of technical and laboratory type interactions that we expect learners to engage with, they can also be easily interpreted for learning experiences that involve field trips and professional practice placements. The guidelines advise that we should arrange elements of what we are designing (or presenting) so as to eliminate or minimise the use of elements that are hazardous, isolated, or hidden. With this, warnings of any hazards and errors, and fail-safe features should be provided. For this principle, the design should discourage any unconscious action in tasks that require vigilance. A useful example of rectifying unintended actions or errors are the various supports that are contained within the menu options of popular word processing packages – for example, the menu option to "Undo Typing" can be used by the user to easily undo the most recent action and revert to the previous version of their work. For many of us, we can identify with this function that can "tolerate error".

Principle Six: Low Physical Effort

The principle of Low Physical Effort guides us to ensure that the service or programme can be used efficiently and comfortably, requiring low physical effort, and with a minimum of fatigue for the learner (Huff, 2020).

Whilst the key reference point here is "physical effort", we can easily understand that this also applies to all forms of effort that could lead to fatigue – for example, excess focus on cognitive load and performance. As noted for principle three, we need to remember that many learners experience difficulties with anxiety, concentration, and other issues that can lead to them feeling overwhelmed quite easily.

The guidelines for this principle advise us that our designs should allow the learner to maintain a neutral body position, entail the use of reasonable operating forces, minimise repetitive actions, and minimise sustained physical effort. Throughout the Covid-19 pandemic, we all experienced a very simple application of this principle. Whilst commonly available in public bathrooms to automate water and soap dispensation, automatic hand sanitisation at the entrances to shops and supermarkets helped to increase sanitisation adherence, increased usability for everyone by eliminating most of the physical effort, and significantly reduced any need for repetitive actions to turn or twist handles or knobs between on and off positions.

Principle Seven: Size and Space for Approach and Use

The final principle reminds us that sufficient size and space should be provided for access and use – that is, approach, reach, manipulation, and use regardless of the learner's body size, posture, or mobility (Huff, 2020).

Aside from obvious anthropometric measurements, a key question for any design is whether it can be used by the greatest number of people possible – without the need for add-ons or amendments. However, UD does facilitate instances where add-ons or amendments are required for some learners. The aspiration is that these modifications would be needed only by a very few individuals – perhaps due to a disability related issue whereby the "reasonable accommodation" to the intervention or programme is necessary.

The guidelines for this principle advise that we provide a clear line of sight to important elements of what we design for any seated or standing learner, ensure that the reach to all components is comfortable for any seated or standing learner, that the design can accommodate variations in hand and grip size, and that we provide adequate space for the use of assistive devices or personal assistance. In higher education, we can often see this principle used in the design of information stations and in the library where the borrowing counter is presented to learners with varying height levels for access. Such variability in height facilitates learners who are either sitting or standing, or who are tall or short. This principle facilitates the opportunity for all learners to access information and services.

Conclusion

In a nutshell, UD supports our "active inclusion" efforts. It seeks to dismantle physical and social barriers to inclusion in all areas of life. When we first think about it, accessibility and UD appears to be a rather straightforward endeavour. However, like most things in life, the reality is a bit more complex than it first appears. UD is the antithesis of a "one size fits all" approach. Done right – with intention – UD goes way beyond what could ever be documented and mandated for in any legislation. Whilst the expression of UD might be guided by principles and guidelines, the implementation of these as "yardsticks rather than templates" should provide each of us in higher education with confidence to reflect upon our own established practices and seek new ways to ensure our services, programmes, and courses are accessible to as many learners as possible. With the understanding of UD gained from this chapter, the next chapter explores how Mace's philosophy and thinking of UD-centred architecture and design has made its way into education.

Points to Consider

Having considered the origin and influences of a UD approach:

- How can you ensure that inclusion for individual differences amongst your learners and colleagues are consciously considered and designed from the outset?

- How confident are you in how the principles outlined in this chapter can be enacted within your practice in higher education?
- Can you identify any UD features in your institution? What are these features and who were they designed for?
- Can you identify anything within your institution that could be redesigned with a UD perspective to allow more learners or colleagues greater access and participation?
- Can you identify an area that you might already be adopting such an approach and reflect on how you might develop this further? What are the opportunities and challenges?

References

American Library Association. (ALA). (2006, December 4). *Universal design. Principles of universal design.* Retrieved from: http://www.ala.org/asgcla/resources/ universaldesign Document ID: dfd141eb-590e-1084-215d-345d2d278cbb

Behling, K. T., & Tobin, T. J. (2018). *Reach everyone, teach everyone: Universal design for learning in higher education.* Morgantown: West Virginia University Press.

Connell, B. R., Jones, M., Mace, R., Mueller, J., Mullick, A., Ostroff, E., Sanford, J., Steinfeld, E., Story, M., & Vanderheiden, G. (1997). *The principles of universal design.* Retrieved from: https://projects.ncsu.edu/ncsu/design/cud/pubs_p/ docs/poster.pdf and www.ncsu.edu/ncsu/design/cud/about_ud/udprinciples text.htm

Huff, D. E. (2020). *Expanding universal design applications within residential homes to maximize person-environment fit for children with intellectual disabilities as they age in place.* (Unpublished Master of Science thesis). University of Oklahoma.

Jones, L. (2010). Accessible, universal, inclusive design: Have the horses reached the finish line? In C. Martin, & D. Guerin (Eds.), *The state of the interior design profession* (pp. 174–179). New York: Fairchild Books.

Mace, R. L. (2008). Ronald L. Mace. Retrieved from: https://projects.ncsu.edu/ ncsu/design/cud/about_us/usronmace.htmdifferences-in-college-persistence-and-retention-rates/

Story, M. F., Mueller, J. L., & Mace, R. L. (1998). *The universal design file: Designing for people of all ages and abilities. Revised Edition.* Retrieved from: https://files.eric.ed.gov/fulltext/ED460554.pdf

Zeng, L. X., & Jiang, X. (2014). Concept analysis of universal design. *CAD/CAM and Manufacturing Informatization, 7,* 25–26.

Chapter 3

Universal Design FOR Learning

Chapter 2 reviewed the foundational philosophy and principles of Universal Design (UD). The seven guiding principles of UD for the fields of architecture and product design have been successfully operationalised beyond these original settings. Increasingly, UD has become the bedrock of various approaches that all extend Mace's original "design for all" thinking to educational contexts.

In this chapter, we present an overview of some approaches that have adapted UD thinking for the educational environment (e.g., Universal Design for Learning, Universal Design for Instruction). In Chapter 4, we will exemplify the most commonly used model that is used in education – the UDL model developed by CAST. Firstly, however, we consider some of the wider educational and social issues that facilitated these developments.

What is notable is the change of language as UD impressed the need to shift from an inclusive education mindset framed predominantly by language related to disability and integration to one of inclusion. The focus pivoted to one of belonging, participation, and equal opportunity – with the key terms being "Universal", "Design", and Inclusion. New research and approaches were developed – each with its own "title". We share in the enthusiasm of colleagues that advocated and developed the thinking in those pioneering years – while recognising that the many new terms and abbreviations can result in inadvertent confusion. Nonetheless, the vision was clear – UD could also work for learning and in learning environments. Inclusion in learning environments was worth designing for.

Extending UD Thinking to Education: Advancing Educational and Social Inclusion

Educational and social inclusion remains a key initiative across higher education, particularly as policies and practices outlined in previous chapters have been embedded, culminating in an increasingly diverse learner population on campus. Various disciplines and courses, especially those with a professional focus, have

DOI: 10.4324/9781003137672-4

increasingly recognised the need to become more accessible to this diversity of learners. We are still seeing the introduction of new widening participation initiatives that are targeted at certain professional disciplines (e.g., teaching).

As our higher education institutions continue to rethink issues related to inclusion, the focus is not only on the learner population. For example, the Athena Swan Charter seeks to support and transform gender equality within higher education and research. In planning for demonstrable actions in all of these active inclusion areas of activity and experience, the application of UD and UDL thinking can help with solutions to previously accepted, yet exclusionary, traditions and practices.

When we expect the world around us to continually change and adapt to new knowledge, we should also challenge ourselves and our higher education institutions to adapt and evolve. The paradox is that whilst higher education can be at the pinnacle of knowledge creation and adventure regarding research endeavours, it can also be one of the most conservative institutions when asked to change well-trodden approaches to teaching, learning, and assessment. It is still amazing that many colleague cling, often unnecessarily, to the traditional essay or lab report as a means to understand learning attainment. It is amazing too to think that whilst many colleagues have moved beyond acetates and markers for the overhead projector, they have become stuck with old and dated slide decks. Many of us probably have colleagues who resolutely refuse to bin their acetates or be visible in online teaching and learning scenarios. Even with the rapid move to online teaching through the Covid-19 pandemic, many have struggled with the idea of having to enable the generation of alt-text for pictures, sub-titles, audio and video recordings, and other inbuilt mechanisms to make learning materials accessible. Whilst many of these software options were originally designed for learners with disabilities, it was very evident through our Covid-19 experience how the majority of learners benefitted from them – for example, the choice to be able to listen to lectures when walking or driving, at a convenient time for the learner, replay at will, and the choice to listen at double-speed.

We are not disputing that it is a challenge to include a greater diversity of learners and colleagues in a system that is continuously evolving. We do acknowledge that academia is on its own journey, continuously developing and considering how it can best keep up with the world in which we live and work in today. To support such educational and social complexities, new and innovative approaches are required. UD and UDL are globally recognisable approaches that can offer great potential to help us all to make sense of inclusive practice in higher education. UD and UDL can offer great support to our changing thinking and practices, presenting an opportunity for higher education to be continually relevant and contemporary.

Increasingly, we are seeing more application of UD and UDL in further and higher education settings. A useful example of a whole sector approach to the application of UDL can be seen in Ireland. The Irish State agency for the

Further Education and Training (FET) sector (SOLAS: www.SOLAS.ie) has recently advanced its "active inclusion" remit by developing a framework of UDL (Quirke & McCarthy, 2020) that can guide UDL practice (Heelan & Tobin, 2021) for everyone working in the Irish FET sector.

We recognise that academic rigour is very important for our community and there is also the "said and unsaid" between theory and practice (i.e., the hidden curriculum). It is a challenge to apply UDL thinking, which was developed with design of tangible products in mind, when greater consideration needs to be given to the fact that learners on campus do not always just learn in a classroom or a lecture hall. This has become even more evident in recent times. Our learners learn in different spaces and different places, meeting and engaging with people that support their learning journey – whether that is the library, the coffee shop, or the clubs and societies across campus. This places an added demand on any inclusion framework for higher education, in that it needs to not just support inclusive practice for a diversity of students in the lecture hall, but must also support a greater inclusion agenda across every part of the campus.

From UD for Disability to UDL

The original philosophy and guiding principles of UD for the built environment and product design have been developed and reimagined into new frameworks for the learning environment. We will introduce and explore some of the better known approaches, describing the thinking behind them, and the challenges of adopting these frameworks in our higher education institutions. However, before exploring these translations of UD into UDL, we first need to revisit the original application of UD thinking to higher education – that is, to support learners with a disability/disabled learners.

The personal testimonies of Patricia McCarthy and Cristina Devecchi at the end of Chapter 1 are useful in our understanding of the influence of the social model of disability and a growing agenda of inclusion across education and society in the latter part of the last century. Interest in equitable access and participation in education, including higher education, increased. So too did interest in what the fresh thinking associated with UD could offer towards the resolution of these challenges. This interest is still very much evident across our higher education institutions, albeit in the guise of UDL rather than UD. Equity to access and participation in higher education is a continual journey rather than a destination. It is not a simple task. There is still a lot to achieve. It is not a done deal!

Being Reflexive

We would encourage you to read and consider these approaches to UDL at a very personal level before thinking about them in terms of your professional practice. All too often we see a rush by colleagues to "do" UDL and implement new approaches to what they do – whether it is in terms of new designs for lectures, curriculum materials, assessments, or wider supports and services in the institution (e.g., the library). A true application of UDL seeks to change hearts and minds. If we expect to change the hearts and minds of others, we must begin with ourselves. We must be reflexive about our current approaches and practices. Being reflexive goes beyond reflection. Reflection is easy – thinking about what we did and whether it worked. Being reflexive takes this a step further – asking further questions that can transform the simple task of remembering and questioning to a more action-oriented approach that seeks to understand what needs to be changed, how to make this change, and how to evaluate the new approach. We need to question our own assumptions, biases, prejudices, and possible discriminatory actions. None of us seeks to make things more complex for our learners, but we often (unintentionally) do when we are not being truly reflexive in our work.

When we see colleagues "doing UDL", we often think that their approaches generate a lot of heat, but not much in terms of illumination! Seeing UDL as some form of checklist activity debases the philosophy of what Mace advocated for in the UD principles. Simply taking one aspect of our work and altering it – albeit with a great intention for it to be more accessible – is not being true to the spirit and ethos of UD/UDL. A more thoughtful approach starts with us engaging in reflexive practice and then exploring the issue with our learners. Why would we seek to change something without asking for input from the end user? Why would we not seek to co-construct new approaches with the "voice" and insider perspective of those that we seek to support with the alterations to our established practices?

A Note About "Universal"

Whilst the term "universal" has the Utopian connotation that it can provide a solution for each and every person, and across each and every situation, the truth is that this is simply not possible. Whilst we can plan and design to be as inclusive as possible from the "get go", there will always be individuals and situations where a truly universal approach is not achievable. We acknowledge this, not as a limitation, but as a recognition of the uniqueness that we all have, and that some individuals will require additional particular and specialised add-ons to what we are planning – whether that is related to teaching, learning, assessment, or the myriad of participation activities (e.g., graduation, clubs and societies, academic registry, library, IT services, catering) that form part of the higher education experience.

Within higher education, the terms "Universal Design" or "UDL" were first used by disability support services. A primary challenge is that while "universal" does imply and mean "a diversity of people" in the context of the term – it has often been thought of as a new approach for including disability. This was perhaps influenced by early thinking behind the research and frameworks developed for education, as these were also grounded in disability practices. UD inspired a number of frameworks for the learning environment and each UD-inspired framework, whether from one factor or a combination of factors, have a primary link to disability. It is important to accept that it does not particularly matter whether a particular framework draws heavily from Maces' architectural design roots, the original principles developed in North Carolina State University, or from differing perspectives of pedagogical practice. The key to fully appreciating and understanding UD and it's subsequent influence in the teaching and learning environment is to first appreciate the issue of inclusion from the position of someone with a disability – someone who may require an add-on (or reasonable accommodation) to enable them to be included, while also recognising how this can set that person apart and make them feel different. Importantly, the concept of UD never set out to be exclusive to disability. Rather, the whole premise of UD is that we should seek, through design, to include everyone who might be excluded through no fault of their own.

A further consideration relates to what the term "universal" might mean across disciplines and global cultures. As we consider the different frameworks and the inclusive practices they inform, we should recognise that no matter the population or applications, they all contribute to a common understanding of inclusive practice across higher education – for an increasing diversity of people. It is this shared understanding of inclusion, together with the fresh thinking and new energy it brings, that can then be exploited. In doing this, we can see deeper links that enable wider applications that go beyond the domains of teaching, learning, and disability in the classroom.

There is much that we do not yet appreciate, as UD, and its application to learning environments, is in its infancy in the context of higher education. However, there is both a plethora of good practice and a growing interest in the principles and practice – and an appreciation of the different frameworks that have led to these developments will serve us well.

Dr Seán Bracken has worked as a teacher, teacher educator, lecturer, and in educational project management across a diversity of settings and jurisdictions, including Samoa, Vanuatu, the US, Ireland, Tonga and, for the past ten years, at the University of Worcester (UW) in England. As Principal Lecturer and Course Coordinator for the National Award SENCO (Special Educational Needs Co Ordinator) with responsibility for Learning and Teaching within the School of Education, Seán is a national and international advocate for UDL and co-edited the highly influential book called *Transforming Higher Education through Universal Design for Learning: An International Perspective*. Seán shares some reflections on some of the challenges a UDL approach faces.

Dr Seán Bracken

As research concerned with Universal Design for Learning (UDL), and Universal Design (UD) more generally, gathers global momentum, a central consideration in this chapter pivots on the question "to what extent can 'Universal Design' be considered as truly universal given its proposed application in a diversity of cultural, socio-economic, and geographical contexts?"

Such a fundamentally important question necessitates a recognition that, while the notions of UD and UDL have their roots in the disability rights movement in the US, the educational and philosophical wellspring of universality, a need to identify what is best for all, is a core consideration manifested in many cultural traditions.

From a European perspective, as early as the 17th century, the great Czech educator Jan Amos Komenský (or Comenius) sought to develop an approach to learning in higher education that was truly universal. His life's challenge, as reflected in the philosophy of "pansophy", was to design a comprehensive approach to sharing all knowledge in ways that were amenable to all learners. This was a mission that was very much grounded in the traditions of the Enlightenment. Of late, two educators from Lithuania, Galkiene and Monkeviciene (2021), have drawn together the strong links between the educational principles underpinning UD and those espoused by Vygotsky, which have in turn informed a growing sense of coherence regarding how inclusive practices might be exemplified within schools (see, for example, Óskarsdóttir, Donnelly, Turner-Cmuchal, & Florian, 2020).

At a time when the inequities of globalisation have prompted powerful populist reactions against liberal principles of inclusion and universality, the ideas presented to us via UD and UDL ignite a sense of urgency for educators from a wide diversity of backgrounds and cultural traditions to come together and forge agreement as to what precisely we mean when using terms such as "universal" or "Universal Design". Following the advice provided by Burgstahler (2020), a productive first step in this process would be to clearly articulate the shared values upon which agreed principles for UD might be constructed. Burgstahler developed her typology to advance UD as a shared institutional strategy. However, there is also a pressing need to clearly articulate how such a shared values base might be more

globally constructed, and how this in turn can inform agreed principles that are actioned in policy and practice.

To a significant degree, that shared imperative is precisely what has
motivated colleagues from across the globe to come together as part
of the International Collaboratory for Leadership in Universally
Designed Education (INCLUDE: https://include.wp.worc.ac.uk/), an
initiative that is still somewhat in its infancy, but one that has an
ambitious but realisable aim to promote collaborative global action
for inclusion. That shared mission should be progressed, not on the
premise of ideological imposition but rather emerging from a
research-informed imperative to ensure that all learners are provided
with all available affordances to realise their inherent learning
potentials, whatever forms of intersectionality may constitute their
learner identities.

The Beginning: Universal Design Moves into Learning

UDL is a multifaceted and nuanced theoretical conceptualisation of learning
that draws upon research from the fields of education, technology, and neuroscience. UDL was initially founded by Anne Meyer and David H. Rose in the
mid-1980s at the non-profit research and development organisation Center for
Applied Special Technology (CAST). Meyer and Rose's initial research interests
were related to the use of technologies and innovative solutions for learning for
students with disabilities. When CAST was founded in 1984, the educational
and social experiences of people with disabilities was completely different than it
is now. Whilst it can be difficult to remember a time when every learner did not
have a smartphone, we must remember that technology in the 1980s was very
new and exciting, and offered opportunities in ways that we had never thought
imaginable. It is also worth reminding ourselves that this was a time when most
learners with disabilities were educated in separate schools and, more often than
not, their peers were also learners who had similar disabilities. This was also a
time when the numbers of learners with disabilities in higher education were
very small. In fact, it was quite extraordinary for someone with a disability to
access and participate in higher education.

Technological advances offered much potential, and this was most particularly evident in educational settings. Whilst assistive technology changed the
educational experience for many learners, most of this was in the form of
individualised add-on supports. It was only when all learners had their own
smartphones and laptops that access to audio books and speech-to-text became
everyday expectations for so many students, irrespective of disability or not.

At about the same time as CAST was establishing itself, Ron Mace and colleagues defined UD and its seven guiding principles at North Carolina State University. The focus was to enable the design of products and buildings that could be usable by all people, to the greatest extent possible, without the need for adaptation of specialised design. By the late 1990s, Rose and Meyer (2002, p. 522) were actively researching and promoting how the use of technology might inform curriculum development so that the experience for learners with disabilities would improve; "the view that 'failure to learn' is not a measure of the inherent capacity of the student but a reflection of learning systems (some part of the systems, such as materials, strategies, policies or infrastructure) that fail to address the needs of all learners". They also stated that each of us has a professional responsibility when designing and developing "learning systems, materials, and environments" to ensure inclusion is undertaken in such a way that it improves professional standards (Rose & Meyer, 2002, p. 524).

Throughout the 1990s, CAST published many papers and shared their thinking about the emerging concept of UDL, with the emphasis now shifting from the individual learner to a whole system approach. While CAST's influential model of UDL was first published in 1998 (Meyer & Rose, 1998), it was not initially targeted at higher education.

Further Developments

As a reaction to the need to include the growing diversity of learners in education, other UD-influenced frameworks emerged. Each of these educationally focused developments of UD thinking has merit, with each making valuable contributions to the growing discourse about inclusive practice and the thinking necessary to achieve it.

Silver, Bourke, and Strehorn (1998), academic professionals, based in Massachusetts carried out a research project where they applied Maces' work – the original UD principles – to postsecondary instructional (teaching/learning) settings. The faculty at a large research university were asked about their experiences combining pedagogical or instructional approaches together with reasonable accommodations used by students with a disability – the exploration resulted in the evolution of the term "Universal Instructional Design" (UID). Their exploratory study is recognised as the first to introduce the concept of Universal Design to a college setting. Although no principles or guidelines for practice were developed from this study for higher education, the work of Silver et al. (1998) was an important contribution as the study explored "inclusive practice" and what it looked like from the perspective of academic teaching staff. This research informed other applications and, most importantly, set about promoting the benefits of the adoption of a UD approach in higher education.

Universal Instructional Design (UID)

Jeanne Higbee commenced her career in student affairs and recognised the beneficial application of UD across all aspects of the higher education campus and its potential to involve all learners in the "inclusive agenda" (2001, 2003, 2004). Higbee's research built upon the work of both Silver et al. (1998) and Ron Mace, developing eight guidelines to support the development of an inclusive approach across post-secondary education. These guidelines aimed to support a great diversity of learners and learning contexts (e.g., traditional classroom, community setting).

Higbee (2001), like her predecessors, advocated for inclusive practices designed for learners with a disability but also to be of benefit for a wide variety of learners. Her focus was predominantly on the term "universal", stating that "[t]he 'universal' in Universal Instructional Design (UID) is not meant to imply that 'one size fits all'; instead, the goal of UID is universal access" (p. 66). Of note, in her work, Higbee identified that student service (as opposed to teaching) needed its own UD approach in recognition of the different but unique role that learner support has on the higher education campus. Services included "(a) counseling or advising, (b) academic support services and developmental education, and (c) administration" (Higbee, 2004, p. 195). The prime focus of her work was on the experience of students outside the class-room and lecture hall. While this focus led to another set of guidelines, ulti-mately Higbee recognises the diverse environment that contributes to the learning experience that is in higher education. This was a proactive response to a growing need for different approaches to inclusion. When considering the application of a design approach, Higbee recognised that each service has its own role and relationship with learners. Higbee (2009) advocated for the benefits of inclusive approaches across the system, stating, "The overlap in ideas and concepts is not unintentional ... a multifaceted institution-wide approach to inclusion ... yet implementing these guidelines in a very intentional way can be transformative" (2004, p. 200).

Universal Design in Education (UDE)

Frank Bowe, a deaf American disability studies academic based at Hofstra University on Long Island, defined "Universal Design in Education" (UDE) as ... "the preparation of curricula, materials, and environments so that they may be used, appropriately and with ease, by a wide variety of people" (Bowe, 2000. p. 45).

As a disability rights activist, author, and teacher, Bowe's thinking was influenced by access to curricular materials, as specified in the legislative framework that guided special education in the US (the 1997 Reauthorization of the Individuals with Disabilities Education Act (IDEA). The UDE guidelines once again embraced the original UD principles developed by Ron Mace and colleagues. Mace's UD principles, together with 31 guidelines from the Centre for Universal Design (CUD) (which looks at the application of Universal Design across a variety of settings in the US), informed Bowes UDE guidelines for post-secondary education settings.

Universal Design for Instruction (UDI)

Scott, McGuire, and Embry (2002) noted that there was an increasing number of higher education learners with apparent and hidden disabilities, alongside other learners who were at risk of academic failure. They noted that the increasing diversity of higher education learners required new approaches if they were to be able to access their learning and achieve their learning goals.

Scott, McGuire, and Foley's (2003) "Universal Design for Instruction" (UDI) presented a nine-principle response to this issue (McGuire, Scott, & Shaw, 2003; Scott, McGuire, & Shaw, 2003). Seven of the principles were adapted from the Centre for Universal Design (CUD), where Mace had developed the original principles for architecture, with the additional two principles in this approach informed by literature relating to successful approaches for learners with varying abilities (Kameenui & Carnine, 1998) and inclusive college teaching practices (Chickering & Gamson, 1987).

McGuire and Scott (2006) developed their UDI approach as part of a federally funded project at the University of Connecticut, advocating that their thinking was grounded in research about best practice in teaching while recognising prior knowledge, building on what teaching staff already know.

Universal Design of Instruction (UDI)

In 2007, Sheryl Burgstahler described "Universal Design of Instruction" (UDI), a concept that also drew on the original UD principles and incorporated instructional examples organised under eight performance indicators. In a similar manner to others who had expanded on the original philosophy and principles of the original UD principles for educational environments, Burgstahler recognised the original UD principles as being the core of how we should think and practice in terms of equality of access and participation. This broader thinking about educational inclusion shifted the focus away from a view that inclusion practices are solely for those learners with a disability, and towards a focus on the unique needs of all learners. In doing this, the focus shifted from the established "add-on" approach to an approach that seeks to design for inclusion from the outset.

As with other approaches, Burgstahler recognised the benefits of each translation of UD to the learning environment, seeing each approach as being complementary rather than in competition. The strength of reflecting on all approaches is that we can see each of the translations of UD for the learning environment co-existing with each other. This 'thinking' lends to a richer, deeper, and wider set of thinking and action tools, increasing the potential for active inclusion, while most importantly lending to a dynamic transformation of culture in academia. This consequently results in changes for each of us with regard to how we think and act "inclusion" in learning environments. Importantly, Burgstahler (2020) reminds us that "[c]hanging habitual behaviour is difficult, even if institutional change to more inclusive design practices may make sense to many people" (p. 178). If each and every one of us accepts the personal challenge to be reflexive, then none of us has to await the institutional lead on these issues. Small changes at the individual level can be motivational and lead to sustained positive change, with the likelihood that colleagues will also seek to change their approach when they observe the success of what you are doing to include.

Commonality across Frameworks

Regardless of the framework that we might be interested in, they each have some common foundations:

- Whilst each framework may have its own approach, they all embrace the necessity to redesign our thinking and adapt our approaches to be more inclusive.
- There is a consensus that higher education requires its own approach, acknowledging the variety of activities that our institutions provide for learners.
- Each framework supports a sustainable and evolving inclusive philosophy. Whilst much of the discourse has evolved from the experience of disability and inclusion in the US, new iterations of the frameworks need to consider new audiences in relation to the culture and experience of inclusion and disability.
- None of the frameworks negate the need for extra individual add-ons where required by learners.
- Each of the frameworks supports the philosophy that inclusion is "everyone's business".

Expanding the Thinking

UDL conceptualises teaching and learning as a dynamic and interactive system that must be reformed to better meet the needs of learners (Rose & Meyer, 2006). At its heart, UDL is about optimising learning and flexible access to the curriculum, emphasising the development of educational materials in various formats to enhance access for all learners, encouraging additional methods of engagement, and developing assessments that accommodate different learners

(Rose & Meyer, 2006; Smith & Lowrey, 2017). In our work, we advocate for a much broader interpretation of UDL. For us, a UDL approach in higher education necessitates thinking that sees the holy trinity of "teaching, learning, and assessment" as only one part of the student experience, with attention also needed to the wider participation and belonging issues that make higher education emancipatory and self-fulfilling for our learners and colleagues.

In seeking to offer equal learning opportunities, UDL is an educational framework that can prove to be an excellent strategy for active and meaningful inclusion, with an ability to create learning environments that offer real opportunities to become expert learners. Expertise through the lens of UDL does not necessarily mean that the learner has an in-depth knowledge of the subject – rather, it accentuates the learner's determination and resourcefulness. Thus, a UDL approach seeks to confront three major challenges that are encountered by all of us in higher education: (i) enhancing diversity, (ii) promoting inclusion in education, and (iii) consciously using technology (Arduini, 2020).

UDL represents a perspective that centres on respect for human diversity-uniqueness, flexibility, real accessibility to learning processes, and recognition and enhancement of the differences of every individual (Savia, 2016). Of central importance to a UDL mindset is the diversity and individual variability to be found among learners (e.g., abilities, preferences, cultures, languages, and experiences) – all of which are important contributing variables to how people learn (Meyer, Rose, & Gordon, 2014).

Adopting a UDL perspective allows you to see the teaching–learning relationship from a different perspective – enabling the optimisation of the curricula to meet the needs of learners. For example:

- UDL can be implemented through the creation of flexible and adaptable curricula;
- UDL can be implemented through a careful analysis of teaching and learning objectives, methods, materials, and assessment during a design phase, taking into account the variety of pupils, regardless of assumed difficulty;
- A UDL approach seeks to guide educational practice which can:
  - Provide flexibility in the format in which information is presented, in the ways in which learners react or demonstrate their knowledge and skills, in the ways in which learners are motivated and involved with their own learning;
  - Reduce barriers in education, provide appropriate adaptations, support and challenge, and maintain high performance expectations for all learners (CAST, 2006);
- UDL does not seek to lower expectations. UDL challenges erroneous assumptions about learner ability – most especially evident in relation to "assumptions" about the ability of learners who have a disability (Arduini, 2020);

- UDL can be used to provide learners with authentic and meaningful opportunities to engage and learn throughout their lives. It also helps teachers to design and implement curriculum that is supportive of all learners from the "get-go", including those with different abilities, needs, or backgrounds.

Developing a Deeper Understanding of All Frameworks

At first glance, each of the frameworks is useful to our work in higher education. However, as with anything that we do, different approaches can lead to different interpretations and actions. We would encourage you to remember that:

1   Each of the different frameworks and approaches uses slightly different terminology. Whilst this is obviously fine, we need to be careful that the core message of designing for inclusion does not get lost or misinterpreted. Different terminology can lead us in slightly different directions of planned action. Some of the terminology used is reflective of underpinning policies, language, and the history of disability. While we need to appreciate different cultures and their stories, we also really need to develop our own understanding of inclusion.

2   There is a growing need to appreciate the issues of efficacy and impact. Developing a UD approach to our roles in higher education requires a research-informed approach. This is vital, as the beneficiaries of our efforts are our learners. We should not be planning and enacting new approaches without some scrutiny. The risk here is that whilst an ad-hoc approach might result in success, this would have been by accident rather than by design. In the absence of a well-planned approach, UDL-inspired approaches may well be seen as just another fad.

3   There are many partners in our UDL work, and there is a role for everyone. We would encourage discussion, inclusion, and collaboration before any planned action. Everyone in a UDL approach has a valuable contribution to make – we all have different experiences and requirements. We need to listen authentically to all partners.

4   While there are several UDL approaches, we also need to recognise the academic diversity that exists across different disciplines, schools, faculties, and services. Each has its own language, terminology, and approaches. Caution is needed here to ensure that everyone is on the same journey and has a shared understanding of the issues and goals. That is, the successful enactment of UDL approaches necessitates a whole community approach.

5   It is evident that much of the thinking behind UDL is influenced by disability. But, there is a growing need to embrace all of our diversities. The risk is that these approaches will only be considered as approaches to disability.

6   As noted in the previous points, all communities on the higher education campus need to share a consistent approach and evolving message of inclusion. Such an interdisciplinary approach will ensure sustainability and a greater chance of success.

Change-Makers

As we reflect on the pioneering efforts of our colleagues to create opportunity and change for learners who have often found themselves challenged by more traditional approaches, it is useful to reflect on their common goal – to create change for inclusion. To enact any meaningful change, we all know that a plan is required. Quite often, our plan is a wish list with some concrete actions. Often there is a large dollop of hope! For our purposes, it is useful at this point to see a valuable approach to project planning. Our colleague, Dr Ke Ren (Rita), successfully uses the well-known Theory of Change (ToC) approach as both a theory and a method to plan for effective policy and practice changes that are informed by research in the early years education sector and from an Early Intervention perspective. Following the very easy to grasp central tenets of ToC can ensure that our efforts to be change-makers will be more likely to be successful.

Dr Ke Ren (Rita)

In my personal work as an early childhood education researcher and practitioner with a special interest in Early Intervention, it is imperative that I embrace both change and diversity on a continuous basis. Across our personal and working lives, we all have great ideas and aims about how the world around us could change for the better. However what we often don't stop to think about is how we are also part of that change.

We continually seek to adopt and adapt newly emerging knowledge. However, because we are always so busy, we rarely take the time to think about what we can do to facilitate positive change and make the world a better place. This is what Quirke, Mc Guckin, and McCarthy (2022) refer to as "Inclusion as Process" – reminding us that whilst we want the world around us to change, we also need to change as part of this process (i.e., it is a bi-directional process).

My own research journey has been influenced by the work of Urie Bronfenbrenner and his observation of the different dynamics at play in our personal developmental ecologies. This led me to also consider using and expanding the Theory of Change (ToC) model in my research (see Ren & Mc Guckin, 2022a).

As Early Intervention involves a diverse range of children, their families, and the professionals who are critically involved in their lives, the emphasis is on relationships. On seeking to include fathers/dads more in these fundamental relationships, a paradigm shift needed to take place. My research identified a need to challenge our beliefs and values pertaining to how we understand the role of the father/dad and their involvement and contribution to the outcomes of their families and children (Ren & Mc Guckin, 2022b).

This is what the ToC process facilitates – mapping backwards from the desired outcomes to determine the outputs and actions required. ToC presents a way of working and thinking, while acknowledging the shared goals of the project. In essence, the ToC enables us to critically reflect on our own values and assumptions, forcing us to make these explicit and actionable. The ToC process demands we take responsibility – rather than do things the way they have always been done.

The challenge as we set about creating change for inclusion is that as we reflect on the learning from our colleagues who have forged ahead and created roadmaps, we recognise that we also need to create our own roadmap. Using a framework designed with another context and goal in mind might not work – nor does following a set of rules realise positive change. We have all tried to follow a healthy eating plan or exercise plan at one time or another, but unless it fits with our lives and the environment we are in, it simply won't realise the results we want! A shared learning UD and all its applications for learning environment highlight is that we need to be and make change. Moreover, we need to make change that supports further positive change – creating a domino effect for inclusion.

Conclusion

This chapter explored some of the UD-inspired approaches that seek to ensure greater inclusion in educational settings. Whilst each approach is both similar and different from each other in terms of how we can operationalise UD thinking, they all demonstrate that inclusive practices are for everyone in our institutions – our learners, our colleagues, and ourselves. Importantly, they all highlight that each and every one of us has a central role to play in developing new ways to help our learners and colleagues to feel and experience active inclusion.

It is an exciting time for higher education. Never has there been such a diversity of thought, practice, and opportunity. It is critical that this is under-pinned by a sustainable agenda of active inclusion.

Points to Consider

As we reflect on the different interpretations of UD in our learning environments, take a moment to explore:

- Were you aware that there are different theories for UD in learning environments?
- How can you adopt a "design thinking" approach in your work – being confident in adopting and adapting the approaches reviewed in this chapter? Is there one framework that works for all? Should there be?
- Does the development of a UDL perspective help you to think about your work for your learners perhaps considering the teaching–learning relationship from a different viewpoint?
- Do you feel you can convince colleagues that UDL is not specific to disability?
- As you reflect on UDL and the different approaches that you have read about, do you have a deeper understanding of what such thinking can mean for higher education and society in the future?

References

Arduini, G. (2020). Curriculum innovation with universal design for learning. *Education Sciences & Society – Open Access, 11*(1), 90–103. Retrieved from: https://ojs.francoangeli.it/_ojs/index.php/ess/article/view/9460. https://doi.org/10.3280/ess1-2020oa9460

Bowe, F. G. (2000). *Universal design in education: Teaching non-traditional students.* Westport, CT: Bergin & Garvey.

Bracken, S., & Novak, K. (Eds.). (2019). *Transforming higher education through universal design for learning: An international perspective.* Routledge.

Burgstahler, S. (2007). Who needs an accessible classroom? *Academe, 93*(3), 37–39. Retrieved from: http://www.jstor.org/stable/40253051

Burgstahler, S. E. (2020). *Creating inclusive learning opportunities in higher education: A universal design toolkit.* Cambridge, MA: Harvard Education Press.

Center for Applied Special Technology. (CAST). (2006). *Universal design for learning (UDL) guidelines version 2.0.* Wakefield, MA: Center for Applied Special Technology.

Chickering, A. W., & Gamson, Z. F. (1987). Seven principles for good practice in undergraduate education. *AAHE Bulletin, 3,* 7. Retrieved from: https://eric.ed.gov/?id=ED282491

Galkiene, A., & Monkeviciene, O. (2021). *Improving inclusive education through universal design for learning.* Springer Nature.

Heelan, A., & Tobin, T. (2021). *UDL for FET practitioners. Guidance for implementing universal design for learning in Irish further education and training.* Dublin, IE: SOLAS & AHEAD Ireland. Retrieved from: https://www.solas.ie/f/70398/x/81044b80ce/fet_practitioners-main.pdf

Higbee, J. L. (2001). Implications of universal instructional design for developmental education. *Research and Teaching in Developmental Education, 17*(2), 67–79. Retrieved from: http://www.jstor.org/stable/42802103

Higbee, J. L. (Ed.). (2003). *Curriculum transformation and disability: Implementing universal design in higher education*. Minneapolis: University of Minnesota, General College, Center for Research on Developmental Education and Urban Literacy.

Higbee, J. L. (2004). Universal design principles for student development programs and services. In J. L. Higbee, & E. Goff (Eds.), *Pedagogy and student services for institutional transformation: Implementing universal design in higher education* (pp. 195–203). University of Minnesota.

Higbee, J. L. (2009). Implementing universal instructional design in postsecondary courses and curricula. *Journal of College Teaching & Learning (TLC)*, *6*(8). https://doi.org/10.19030/tlc.v6i8.1116

Kameenui, E. J., & Carnine, D. W. (1998). *Effective teaching strategies that accommodate diverse learners*. Prentice Hall.

McGuire, J. M., & Scott, S. S. (2006). Universal design for instruction: Extending the universal design paradigm to college instruction. *Journal of Postsecondary Education and Disability*, *19*(2), 124–134.

McGuire, J. M., Scott, S. S., & Shaw, S. F. (2003). Universal design for instruction: The paradigm, its principles, and products for enhancing instructional access. *Journal of Postsecondary Education and Disability*, *17*(1), 11–21.

Meyer, A., & Rose, D. (1998). Learning to read in the computer age. In J. Chall (Series Ed.), & J. Onofrey (Ed.), *From reading research to practice*. Cambridge, MA: Brookline Books.

Meyer, A., Rose, D. H., & Gordon, D. (2014). *Universal design for learning: Theory and practice*. Boston, MA: CAST Professional Publishing.

Óskarsdóttir, E., Donnelly, V., Turner-Cmuchal, M., & Florian, L. (2020). Inclusive school leaders–their role in raising the achievement of all learners. *Journal of Educational Administration*, *58*(5), 521–537. https://doi.org/10.1108/JEA-10-2019-0190

Quirke, M., & McCarthy, P. (2020). *A conceptual framework of universal design for learning (UDL) for the Irish further education and training sector: Where inclusion is everybody's business*. Dublin, IE: SOLAS & AHEAD Ireland. Retrieved from: https://www.solas.ie/f/70398/x/b1aa8a51b6/a-conceptual-framework-of-universal-design-for-learning-udl-for-the-ir.pdf

Quirke, M., Mc Guckin, C., & McCarthy, P. (2022). How to adopt an "inclusion as process" approach and navigate ethical challenges in research. In *SAGE research methods cases*. London, UK: SAGE Publications, Ltd. https://doi.org/10.4135/9781529605341

Ren, K., & Mc Guckin, C. (2022a). Using theory of change as both theory and method in educational research. In *SAGE research methods cases*. London, United Kingdom: SAGE Publications, Ltd. https://doi.org/10.4135/9781529601596

Ren, K., & Mc Guckin, C. (2022b). The role and involvement of dads in the lives and education of their children with special educational needs and/or disabilities within an early intervention context. *Education Thinking*, *2*(1), 3–18. ISSN 2778-777X

Rose, D. H., & Meyer, A. (2002). *Teaching every student in the digital age: Universal design for learning*. Alexandria, VA: Association for Supervision and Curriculum Development (Product no. 101042).

Rose, D. H., & Meyer, A. (Eds.). (2006). *A practical reader in universal design for learning.* Cambridge, MA: Harvard Education Press.

Savia, G. (2016). *Universal design for learning. Progettazione universale per l'apprendimento e didattica inclusiva.* Trento: Erickson.

Scott, S., McGuire, J. M., & Embry, P. (2002). *Universal design for instruction fact sheet.* Storrs: University of Connecticut, Center on Postsecondary Education and Disability.

Scott, S. S., McGuire, J. M., & Foley, T. E. (2003). Universal design for instruction: A framework for anticipating and responding to disability and other diverse learning needs in the college classroom. *Equity & Excellence in Education, 36*(1), 40–49. https://doi.org/10.1080/10665680303502

Scott, S. S., McGuire, J. M., & Shaw, S. F. (2003). Universal design for instruction: A new paradigm for adult instruction in postsecondary education. *Remedial and Special Education, 24*(6), 369–379. https://doi.org/10.1177/074193250302-0 060801

Silver, P., Bourke, A., & Strehorn, K. C. (1998). Universal instructional design in higher education: An approach for inclusion. *Equity & Excellence in Education, 31*(2), 47–51. https://doi.org/10.1080/1066568980310206

Smith, S., & Lowrey, K. (2017). Making the UDL framework universal: Implications for individuals with intellectual disability. *Intellectual and Developmental Disabilities, 55*(1), 2–3. https://doi.org/10.1352/1934-9556-55.1.2

Chapter 4

The CAST Model of UDL

From an educational and social inclusion perspective, there is an ongoing and increasing need to develop equitable learning and work environments – creating a world of learning where individual differences between, and among, people are appreciated – moreover, a place where all learners can thrive and demonstrate their full potential. In support of this goal, Chapter 3 introduced a variety of Universal Design (UD) frameworks that have been developed for the educational environment. Whilst it can always be easy to "compare" and "contrast" such approaches, each approach shares one critical thing in common – a wish to implement a positive and proactive "inclusion" agenda. Rather than developing a detailed critique of these approaches, we want to use this chapter to introduce you to the model of UDL that has the broadest appeal – the CAST model of Universal Design for Learning (UDL). Influenced by the seven principles of UD, the CAST model of UDL was developed by a multidisciplinary team in the US, led by David Rose and Anne Meyer. Initially focused on issues related to assistive technology for learners with a disability, the model was named after the Center for Applied Special Technology.

As you read through this chapter, we would encourage you to use the CAST model as a foundation from which to think about – and challenge – your own knowledge and attitude towards inclusion for your higher education role. We argue that implementing UDL as a simple hands-on toolkit underestimates the power of the approach. That is, we encourage you to move beyond seeing the application of the model as a checklist. All too often we have heard colleagues declare that they have used the model and have "UDL'd" something – for example, changed a module assessment. Without some personal and professional reflection, the danger is that any UDL approach will become a checklist or template approach to what we do. The inherent risk here, is that such an approach will unconsciously result in exclusionary practice once again.

Thinking and practicing active inclusion is a challenge. Too many colleagues do not take the time to think about the reasons why they might take a UDL approach in their work. To be successful, you need to have faith, in both yourself and in others. When implemented in an authentic and sustainable way,

DOI: 10.4324/9781003137672-5

there are great rewards to be had. Adopting a positive mindset and attitude necessitates not just change but a need to adopt the very features that make the CAST model of UDL so alluring.

Beginning a UDL journey requires us to ask questions. Rudyard Kipling's "Six Honest Serving Men" might help you here – their names are: Who and What and When and Where and Why and Which. Some initial prompt questions might include the following:

- **"Who"** is being challenged?
  - Who is experiencing the problem?
  - Who can offer a solution?
  - Are there multiple "who's" in the problem and solution?
- **"What"** is the barrier or issue that is being faced?
  - What is it that you are being asked to do?
  - What would you like to see happen?
  - What could facilitate change?
- **"When"** did the problem start?
  - Who identified the problem – you or the learner?
  - Was this always a problem, or did it start after a previous change to what you were doing?
  - When can you start the process?
- **"Where"** do you begin?
  - Where can you find support or an example of good practice?
  - Where can you find good reference materials?
  - Where can you find colleagues to share ideas with?
- **"Why"** should you do anything at all?
  - Consider why should it be you to do this – is it your issue to resolve
  - Why change if it already works for most of your learners?
  - Why change if it already meets the necessary standards?
- **"Which"** parts of the UDL framework do you most readily identify with
  - Which parts do you want to explore further?
  - Which part should you try first?
  - Which part of current practice has led to your thinking about using UDL?

In our own work in higher education, we always try to start with a brainstorming session to explore these simple question prompts. In doing so, we use the CAST model "as a yardstick rather than as a template". In doing so, this stops us from rushing ahead and seeing each problem as being somewhat similar to a previous issue that we have worked on, and then making lazy and erroneous assumptions that if X approach worked for Y setting and problem, then X will likely also work in this new setting for Z.

In the next section, we will present an outline of the basic infrastructure of the CAST model of UDL. Following this, we will present a personal reflection of how one of our Irish colleagues (Mags Flood) has used the model, as well as her reflections on a recent Fulbright Scholarship to travel to, and engage with, people working at CAST in 2021. Mags' commentary is both useful and encouraging to any of us about to embark on a new UDL journey!

The CAST Model of UDL: Three Pillars – the Cornerstone of Inclusion!

CAST propose their model of UDL is deeply rooted in the learning sciences, with pedagogical, neuroscientific, and practice bases. The model identifies three different interconnected learning brain networks: neural recognition networks, strategic neural networks, and affective neural networks (Arduini, 2020), each of which provides the underlying structure for the three founding pillars of the UDL Guidelines, which will be discussed subsequently.

Whilst the model is continually updated to reflect the latest knowledge from disparate disciplines, it very usefully reflects contemporary social and equality-based issues that affect the diversity of learners that we encounter – for example, Black Lives Matter. Much of the focus of the CAST model has been upon applications to teaching, learning, and assessment in the post-primary education classroom. However, the utility of the model is that it is easily understood and applicable by any of us involved in education – whether we work in an academic registry, a library, information services, or laboratories, or perform teaching activities.

The perennial success of the CAST model rests in its ability to convey so much useful information and planning approaches in a very accessible manner. The model becomes very easy to apply to practice, often seeming very intuitive. Many readers initially get excited by seeing some aspect of the model that they are already enacting in practice. However, the important thing to remember is that this application of a UDL principle has often been done by chance – and not with intent. The model is flexible and allows any of us involved in higher education to build upon our own knowledge and expertise, facilitating a fresh look at our practices, and encouraging us to re-design our thinking to create learning environments that are as inclusive of as many people as possible, from the get-go.

CAST's model of UDL is directed by three inter-related "Pillars", each focused around a set of "Guidelines" and associated "Checkpoints" for action, whereby flexibility is key in terms of teaching, learning, assessment, and the wider learning environment:

Pillar 1: **Multiple Means of Engagement** (the "why" of learning: affective neural networks) – enabling learners to engage positively with their learning and to appreciate the value of learning;

Pillar 2: **Multiple Means of Representation** (the "what" of learning: neural recognition networks) – focusing on offering choice in learning;

Pillar 3: Multiple Means of Action/Expression (the "how" of learning: strategic neural networks) – considering assessment as part of the process, so that learners have a very real choice in how they represent their learning (e.g., multiple options – not just an essay) while meeting curriculum goals and learning outcomes.

Usefully, each of these three Pillars is sub-divided into three sets of Guidelines, each with its own set of Checkpoints to help us in our thinking and planning. Cutting across the 3 Pillars, the Guidelines are also usefully related to the areas of "access" (i.e., linking the Guidelines that suggest ways in which we can increase the learner's access to learning), "build" (i.e., those Guidelines that suggest ways in which we can help learners to develop their effort and persistence), and "internalise" (i.e., the Guidelines that suggest how we can empower the learner). We will explore the simplicity and usefulness of each of these in the subsequent sections. As noted earlier, these parts of the framework are not to be considered as a rigid prescription of rules or strategies to be applied or valid for every occasion. Rather, they are designed to help prompt us to consider our work and what we can all do to develop maximum flexibility for our learners, with the end-goal being a learning environment whereby learners can maximise learning opportunities.

Pillar 1: Provide Multiple Means of Engagement

The focus of Pillar 1 is on providing the learner with multiple means of engaging with their learning tasks. The ambition here is to help the learner become motivated and enthused about their learning by promoting various ways (multiple means) in which they can engage with the tasks associated with their learning. As we all know, motivated learners engage positively with their learning.

This Pillar, derived from research knowledge about affective neural networks, underlines that affectivity, and in general emotionality, is the basis of the learning process. Numerous studies highlight the link between motivation (extrinsic or intrinsic), positive climate, and aptitude for learning. Whilst some learners might be motivated by the novelty of a new learning task, others might prefer the same old routine. Other learners might prefer to work in a group or, on the contrary, alone. Consequently, there is no single way of involvement that applies to every learner and in all contexts. For example, when we consider our own daily tasks at work, we easily identify our own individual preferences for how we work, compared to colleagues.

So, when we think about providing multiple means of engagement, we could consider how it might be possible to plan for additional activities that learners participate and demonstrate achievements in relation to curricula learning outcomes. The goal of this Pillar is to have "expert learners who are purposeful and motivated".

Increasing Access – Recruiting Interest

For Pillar 1 (Provide Multiple Means of Engagement), "Access" relates to how we can provide options for "Recruiting Interest" (CAST's Guideline 7). CAST note that whilst considerable effort is always made in terms of recruiting learner attention and engagement, sometimes important information either is not attended to or does not sufficiently stimulate the learner to pay attention to it. Thus, this information becomes "inaccessible". This is not an easy issue to resolve. There are, of course, individual differences between learners in their preferences for how learning materials are presented to them. Indeed, even at the individual level, our own preferences are not static – generally becoming more dynamic as we move from novice to expert learners. For us, the key thinking that is needed here relates to how we can make our information accessible through the creation of a variety of means (or materials) that can stimulate learner interest. To assist us in our thinking and planning, CAST provide three Checkpoints for this Guideline: (i) optimise individual choice and autonomy (Checkpoint 7.1), (ii) optimise relevance, value, and authenticity (Checkpoint 7.2), and (iii) minimise threats and distractions (Checkpoint 7.3).

Building and Developing Expertise – Sustaining Effort and Persistence

For Pillar 1 (Provide Multiple Means of Engagement), "Build" relates to how we can provide options for "Sustaining Effort & Persistence" (CAST's Guideline 8). For our learners in higher education, we expect them to learn concepts, theories, research methods, skills, and strategies for applied practice. Our courses are generally not short, and mastery of the topic matter requires sustained attention, concentration, and effort. As mentioned earlier, we know that learners who are motivated – and remain motivated – will be successful. This Guideline helps us to consider how we can help our learners to develop and sustain their self-determination, as well as their ability to self-regulate (i.e., to understand and manage emotions so that we can be more effective at coping with stressors in our environment). We spoke earlier about using Rudyard Kipling's honest servants – how would you use those prompts to help you with this task? You could also explore the prompts provided by CAST in the four Checkpoints for this Guideline: (i) heighten salience of goals and objectives (Checkpoint 8.1), (ii) vary demands and resources to optimise challenge (Checkpoint 8.2), (iii) foster collaboration and community (Checkpoint 8.3), and (iv) increase mastery-oriented feedback (Checkpoint 8.4).

Empowering the Learner – Self-Regulation

For Pillar 1 (Provide Multiple Means of Engagement), "Internalise" relates to how we can provide options for "Self-Regulation" (CAST's Guideline 9).

Extending the importance of learner self-determination and self-regulation noted above, this issue requires us to think more holistically about the learner and their development – not simply seeing them in terms of participation activities and associated assessments. We all differ in our ability to self-regulate. This is what makes us unique in terms of our psychological development and how we process and respond to the world around us. Many of us find this task difficult – either intermittently in acute episodes or more chronically as part of our dispositions. Our learners are no different, and for some learners, this is an area of life that is a constant struggle.

Rather than simply ignoring the internal world of the learner, CAST encourage us here to stop and think about how these internal issues can affect motivation, engagement, and performance. In terms of this Pillar's focus on "multiple means", the task for all of us here is to make self-regulation an explicit issue in our work – not something that is, or should be, ignored. If we acknowledge that we all have different experiences and abilities in relation to self-regulation, our task relates to how we can increase the ways in which we can support our learners to effectively manage their own engagement and affect. Can you think of an area of your work where an acknowledgement of self-regulation, and its impact on motivation and performance, can be altered to help your learners? From Heelan and Tobin's (2021) advice, could you develop a "plus one" approach – identify just one area of practice where you could create just one more way of doing something that is currently done?

CAST's three Checkpoints for this Guideline can be useful too: (i) promote expectations and beliefs that optimise motivation (Checkpoint 9.1), (ii) facilitate personal coping skills and strategies (Checkpoint 9.2), and (iii) develop self-assessment and reflection (Checkpoint 9.3).

Pillar 2: Provide Multiple Means of Representation of Content

The focus of Pillar 2 is to offer choice to the learner around their learning. Developed from research knowledge about the neural networks of recognition, this Pillar reminds us that, just like our learners, we all differ in how we perceive the information that we need for our jobs. Information that we need to complete an assignment might be presented to us in different ways – sometimes in written format, perhaps in an auditory format at other times, or maybe visually sometimes – or perhaps even a mixture of these formats. Depending on how the material is presented, each of us might find it either easier or more difficult to attend to the information and understand what we need to do with it. Again, we can see that individual differences exist amongst us all. And this is even before we might consider that some of us might have a disability and/or additional learning requirement that could be important in relation to how the information is presented. Coupled with these factors, our higher education institutions are increasingly international, and we can understand how language and cultural issues could also have an importance here. For example, Conor detests the auditory mode because it seems to lack the visual imagery that can help Conor to make a connection with the task and the people that need the job done. On the other hand, because of her sight issues, Patricia has a preference for information to be presented in auditory format – or maybe enlarged print format using some extra technology to assist. Thus, in this Pillar of UDL, CAST remind us that there is not simply one way of representing information (i.e., "representation") that will be ideal for all of our learners, and that a useful approach would see us using multiple representations and exploiting all five senses, so as to provide learners with different and multiple options for acquiring information.

So, when we think about providing multiple means of representation of content, we have the goal of helping our learners to become "expert learners who are resourceful and knowledgeable".

Increasing Access – Perception

For Pillar 2 (Provide Multiple Means of Representation), "Access" relates to how we can provide options for "Perception" (CAST's Guideline 1). The issue of perception is closely related to the concepts of attention, memory, and retrieval. If we were to look at those few words in reverse order, we can see the importance of how we perceive information both in our environment and learning activities.

For example, all aspects of learning require us to be able to retrieve the correct information from our memory, without errors in recall. We have all had experiences of the failure that we can have when trying to retrieve some information that we have previously learnt and stored away in memory for future use. Indeed, we tend to use memory aids to make retrieval more successful. For example, some use mnemonics to rehearse and remember key information. As children, many of us rehearsed the rhyme that "Richard of York Gave Battle in Vain", with the first letter of each word in the rhyme representing a colour of the rainbow: red, orange, yellow, green, blue, indigo, and violet. Similarly, many of us might have mastered the letters for sin(e), cos(ine), and tan(gent) in trigonometry at school by remembering that "Oliver Had A Handful of Apples": O/H (sin: opposite divided by hypothenuse), A/H (cos: adjacent divided by hypothenuse), O/H (tan: opposite divided by adjacent). Thus, retrieving information becomes easier if we can memorise and store it correctly in either short- or long-term memory.

However, nothing can be stored if we cannot attend to it in the first place. To be able to attend to information, it needs to be presented to us in a manner that makes it easy for us to perceive and attend to. As humans with five senses, we are constantly bombarded every second with all types of sensory information. As we have a limited attention span and a limited storage capacity in our brains, we unconsciously disregard a vast amount of information that we get through our senses. If we stop the task that we are currently doing, we can start to perceive and attend to information that we were not even aware of previously – for example, the ticking of the clock, traffic noise from outside. So, it makes sense that we will be able to perceive and attend to information that is valuable to us if it is presented in a very perceptible manner. Being able to perceive and attend to information means that we can rehearse and store it for later recall and action.

From a UDL perspective, the process of learning becomes impaired if the information that we need to attend to and learn is presented in formats that require a lot of effort. To reduce barriers to learning, the CAST model guides us to ensure that key information is equally perceptible to all learners by: (i) providing the same information in different formats (e.g., visual, auditory, tactile), (ii) providing the information in a format that can be adjusted by the user (e.g., text that can be enlarged, auditory information that can be amplified). By having such "multiple representations", we are helping all of our learners – not only those with a disability and/or additional learning requirement.

Recognising these differences in perception and utilising different approaches to the presentation of information (e.g., different font sizes and colours, graphics, images, videos, hyperlinks to glossaries, iPad, black/whiteboard) can enhance learner attention and motivation to engage in the learning process – thus helping them become "experts by experience". This is the true essence of a UDL approach – designing from the get-go to be useable, with ease, by the greatest number of learners. Within this Guideline, CAST provide us with three Checkpoints: (i) offer ways of customising the display of information (Checkpoint 1.1), (ii) offer alternatives for auditory information (Checkpoint 1.2), and (iii) offer alternatives for visual information (Checkpoint 1.3).

Building and Developing Expertise – Language and Symbols

For Pillar 2 (Provide Multiple Means of Representation), "Build" relates to how we can provide options for "Language & Symbols" (CAST's Guideline 2). As the poet John Donne reminds us, "no man is an island" (John Donne, 1572–1631: Devotions upon Emergent Occasions). Donne's words remind us that, as humans, we are *the* social animal – seeking out the comfort, support, and companionship of other humans. Central to this common desire is the need to communicate – both in language and symbols. We can all remember instances where we have ended up in trouble due to a misunderstanding of what someone has asked us to do, or where we have mis-interpreted a sign or symbol. This serves to remind us that none of us is perfect – either in communicating or in receiving a message. With this personal reflection, we are reminded here that our learners are no different.

What might appear to be clear to us might be exceptionally difficult and a challenge for the learner. This can happen very easily in higher education, where each subject area and discipline has its own specific language and terminology (and perhaps symbols), and where we need to remember that what might be a normal part of conversation for us as experts in a discipline, can be difficult for the novice. Added to this, some of our learners have communication difficulties, and some learners are from different cultural and linguistic backgrounds. Even the most basic level of participation can be fraught with difficulties related to understanding spoken language and the local dialect that each of us likely has. Whilst the language and symbols (e.g., notations, graphs) that we use might make some concepts crystal clear for some learners, the opposite could be true for others.

In this Guideline, CAST remind us that inequalities arise when information is presented to all learners through a single form of representation. To support the diversity of our learners, we should constantly seek to ensure that alternative representations are provided – not only for accessibility, but for clarity and comprehensibility. Within this Guideline, CAST provides us with five Checkpoints: (i) clarify vocabulary and symbols (Checkpoint 2.1); (ii) clarify syntax and structure (Checkpoint 2.2); (iii) support decoding of text, mathematical notation, and symbols (Checkpoint 2.3); (iv) promote understanding across languages (Checkpoint 2.4); and (v) illustrate through multiple media (Checkpoint 2.5).

Empowering the Learner – Comprehension

For Pillar 2 (Provide Multiple Means of Representation), "Internalise" relates to how we can provide options for "Comprehension" (CAST's Guideline 3). In the previous Guidelines, there was quite a bit of attention directed at issues related to how we can present information to our learners in a more accessible manner; providing such information in multiple formats. Similarly, we were guided to remember that learners also have preferences for how they output information and learning – with learners expressing individual differences in how they might wish to demonstrate their learning. For this next Guideline, the focus moves to how we can help the learner internalise information. That is, how we can use UDL approaches to help them transform our accessible information into knowledge. This is, after all, the hallmark of what we want our learners to be able to do in their higher education studies.

Drawing upon research from cognitive psychology (e.g., the information processing approach) and educational pedagogy (e.g., constructivist approaches to learning), this Guideline serves to remind us that learning is an active and participatory process. Many of our programme and module learning outcomes reflect these higher order cognitive capabilities. We expect learners to synthesise and integrate new information with previous course knowledge. From a Vygotskyian perspective, we can scaffold the learner and help them to extend their knowledge and confidence by how we structure our learning sessions.

Indeed, success in higher education goes far beyond the lecture hall and the assessment processes.

Our learners participate in sports activities, clubs and societies, and graduation ceremonies. They also draw heavily on the myriad of services and opportunities that many higher educational institutions provide – including the library and information services, academic registry, student health and counselling services, careers and disability services, IT services, catering and social life, and estates management. For all of us, we need to ensure that we seek to apply UDL thinking to all of these points of learner engagement. If we do not, there will be a disconnect between the traditional UDL application to teaching, learning, and assessment, with exclusionary practices evident in other points of the higher education experience. In your role, can you recognise any aspects of your own practice, or that of your colleagues, that could benefit from thinking about the focus of this Guideline? As with the other Guidelines, CAST provide Checkpoints to help us tease out these issues: (i) activate or supply background knowledge (Checkpoint 3.1); (ii) highlight patterns, critical features, big ideas, and relationships (Checkpoint 3.2); (iii) guide information processing and visualisation (Checkpoint 3.3); and (iv) maximise transfer and generalisation (Checkpoint 3.4).

Pillar 3: Provide Multiple Means of Action and Expression

The focus of Pillar 3 is to ensure that learners can navigate the learning environment, and demonstrate their knowledge and understanding. Drawing upon research knowledge about our strategic neural networks, this Pillar seeks to remind us that we all express knowledge in different ways, and that this becomes really important when we consider the diversity that exists among our learners (e.g., disability, language, self-regulation, organisation, and executive function issues).

None of us is the same – not by a long shot. For example, even though they share similar genetic, environmental, and cultural backgrounds, siblings can learn in ways that are very different from each other (Hartmann, 2015; Rose & Meyer, 2006). Rose and Meyer (2006) point to research from the learning sciences and neurology that has found that all learners, even those who come from similar cultural backgrounds and have similar abilities, can vary greatly in how they approach learning tasks (Rose & Meyer, 2006).

Many of our higher education courses still rely heavily on examining learner knowledge through the classic methods of expression – written and oral tests. Whilst some of us might be able to express ourselves very eloquently in oral examination situations, some of us might prefer to draft an essay or a report. When you think about it, it seems very restrictive to assess knowledge and understanding with only these approaches – especially considering the contemporary world that we live in and the tools of modernity that we could allow learners to use so that they can fully express what they know, in a format that makes sense to them. In our experience, when different expressive actions are facilitated, we often see surprisingly effective results, reminding us that there is no one means of action and expression valid for all learners.

It should, therefore, not be beyond us to enable each learner to develop and then express their knowledge in different formats. We already do this when we allow learners to use assistive technology and produce assignment and examination work in alternative formats. With wider application of the principle, many other learners may become more engaged and motivated in their learning process and produce excellent work that would not be possible with a more homogenous approach to assessment. So, when we think about providing multiple means of action and expression, we have the goal of helping our learners to become "strategic and goal-directed".

Increasing Access – Physical Action

For Pillar 3 (Provide Multiple Means of Action and Expression), "Access" relates to how we can provide options for "Physical Action" (CAST's Guideline 4). Central to learner success is the ability to access the teaching curriculum and associated materials. So too is the ability to physically access all of the other aspects of the higher education campus that support the learning journey and experience. Whilst some issues are naturally dealt with through UD principles in that they promote accessibility by way of good design in the built environment and products – many of us have a significant role to play in removing physical access barriers.

At a practical level, we can easily see how this issue can be related to learning materials. For example, many courses rely on learners accessing information that is presented in hardcopy books. These require manual dexterity to handle them and turn their pages. Even when we see these resources presented in a digital format, there can be attendant issues with the need for particular hardware requirements or the ability to use these. For some of our learners, a UDL approach must be supplemented with an assistive technology solution. When we design things like our courses, advertising brochures, assessments, and forms that need to be completed, have we always considered these access issues?

Through the recent Covid-19 pandemic, we very quickly saw the application of technology and approaches that were previously only considered for learners with a disability being useful for everyone. We have all become used to seeing alt(ernative) text accompanying visual images, functions on video conferencing tools to help us all feel more included, videos, and podcasts. So perhaps it is easier than we first thought to be creative and imaginative with how we make our resources more varied and accessible – with lots of choice for the learner. To nudge our thinking in relation to this Guideline, CAST provide two very useful Checkpoints: (i) vary the methods for response and navigation (Checkpoint 4.1) and (ii) optimise access to tools and assistive technologies (Checkpoint 4.2).

Building and Developing Expertise – Expression and Communication

For Pillar 3 (Provide Multiple Means of Action & Expression), "Build" relates to how we can provide options for "Expression & Communication" (CAST's Guideline 5). Being able to communicate effectively about ongoing and completed learning is fundamental to learner success in higher education. However, we already recognise that whilst some of our learners might be great at verbally presenting their ideas and work, these same learners can really struggle with presenting the same information in written format (e.g., dyslexia). Therefore, where possible, we should explore how we can help the learner to effectively express and communicate their learning. As before, do we always need the expression and communication to be text based? As our courses and campuses become more contemporary and modern, reflecting the society and disciplines that we seek to influence, then surely we also need to be more open to the tools and techniques of communication that we have in everyday life outside of the campus. This Guideline reminds us that there is no single medium of expression that is equally useful for all learners or for all kinds of communication. CAST's Checkpoints provide thinking approaches for us to consider: (i) use multiple media for communication (Checkpoint 5.1); (ii) use multiple tools for construction and composition (Checkpoint 5.2); and (iii) build fluencies with graduated levels of support for practice and performance (Checkpoint 5.3).

Empowering the Learner – Executive Functions

For Pillar 3 (Provide Multiple Means of Action & Expression), "Internalise" relates to how we can provide options for "Executive Functions" (CAST's Guideline 6). Executive function and self-regulation skills really showcase our ability to plan ahead, focus our attention, remember and adhere to the detail in instructions, monitor our performance, modify performance if needed, and tackle multiple tasks simultaneously. As an analogy, we can think of an example where the individual is the conductor of an orchestra that is comprised of the various executive functions. With a good conductor, and with all of the various sections of the orchestra turning up for work and playing their part as directed, we hear some gorgeous music. Unfortunately, not everyone is a great conductor, and for some people, they might be struggling with getting the most out of some members of the orchestra.

From a UDL perspective, if we are getting our learners to spend too much time and attention on resolving some of the lower level activities and issues that we have explored previously, that could become easier and more fluid if we enacted "multiple means" – then these learners would have more executive function capacity freed up for higher level tasks. We need to remember too that some learners, because of a disability or cognitive impairment, will experience difficulty with some executive function tasks.

CAST's framework of UDL continually seeks to support the development of executive functioning by reducing the learner's cognitive burden. In some of the Guidelines and Checkpoints reviewed earlier, we have seen how UDL interventions can serve to reduce the required amount of cognitive processing, thus freeing up capacity for higher order thinking and performance (i.e., executive functioning). As with the other Guidelines, CAST provide Checkpoints to help us tease out these and develop appropriate responses to this important issue: (i) guide appropriate goal-setting (Checkpoint 6.1), (ii) support planning and strategy development (Checkpoint 6.2), (iii) facilitate managing information and resources (Checkpoint 6.3), and (iv) enhance capacity for monitoring progress (Checkpoint 6.4).

We asked our good colleague Dr. Mags Flood to provide her perspective on the CAST model of UDL. Dr. Flood is the Education Officer for Inclusive Education and Diversity at the Ireland's National Council for Curriculum and Assessment (NCCA), and was a Fulbright Irish Scholar Awardee to visit and work with colleagues at CAST in 2021.

Dr Mags Flood

UDL was developed by CAST in the mid-1980s. Based in neuroscience and the learning potential of the brain, UDL is an inclusive pedogeological approach that provides UDL guidelines as a tool to enact inclusive practices. UDL takes the stance that barriers to learning come from the environment, including curriculum design, and not from within the learner – thus pushing educators to change how they view the learners in their environments and, in turn, how they design for and with them (CAST, n.d.; Meyer, Rose, & Gordon, 2014). While it can be argued that more evidence-based research is required on the effectiveness of UDL (e.g., Capp, 2017), there is evidence of UDL gaining momentum across all of the Irish education sectors (Flood & Banks, 2021).

Here, I reflect on what I consider to be the main reasons for UDL's growing appeal in Ireland, and internationally.

1   UDL is a move away from thinking in terms of ability and disability to thinking in terms of variability. This, for me, is the hook that reels us in, and Meyer at al.'s foundational book *Universal Design for Learning: Theory and Practice* is based on this premise. Neuroscience has already taught us that every brain learns differently, and that we use different parts of the brain for

different learning processes (CAST, 2018), regardless of ability or disability. This is why we, as educators, need to stop thinking about our learner groups in terms of categories (bright, average, Autistic, intellectual disability, blind, etc.) and assigning support or challenge based on what we think is the right approach for that group of learners. Instead, we need to think about variability. Variability in terms of the diversity of learners we are designing for, regardless of a pre-assigned "label", and the variability within each learner. If we recognise the jagged profile (Rose, 2016) of each individual, we can begin to design for the individual and not the subject or topic. This does not mean more work. In fact, once we begin to change our way of thinking we realise that variability is, for the most part, predictable and with intentional design we will be able to predict what options, support, and challenges to incorporate into particular learning experiences. For me, I have my own toolbox of strategies. I don't put them all into every design. Rather, I choose what will work best in the context of a particular learning experience, and I do this through co-designing – but that is for another conversation.

2   The barriers to learning come from outside, not within. Thinking in terms of variability pushes us to think outside the box and outside the learner. We accept that the barriers to learning are the environment, curriculum design, and, in some cases, us – the educators. This enables us to identify the barriers to learning in various contexts and apply the UDL Guidelines to help remove them.

3   UDL is goal orientated. As educators, we know our learning goals and our learning intentions, but because we know them so well, we forget to clarify them for our learners. This can create barriers to their learning – because of implicit tasks or additional skills we have unconsciously built into it (Meyer et al., 2014; Posey & Novak, 2020). For UDL, it is crucial to know our goals, to be clear when designing our lesson about what the purpose of the learning experience is for our learners, and to communicate this clearly to our learners. When we set clear and rigorous goals, we can anticipate the challenges that create barriers that may prevent our learners from achieving the goal. With this clarity and knowledge, we can intentionally design for student options because we know where and how we can be flexible (Posey & Novak, 2020) and we can remove unnecessary means within the task design. Consider this in terms of the goal "to

demonstrate safe laboratory procedures". We could instruct our learners to watch a video on laboratory safety, take notes, and study for a quiz before they can work in the laboratory. But is that the goal? Does a quiz facilitate our learners to demonstrate their knowledge, understanding, and skills in laboratory safety procedures? Did we design, for example, for the concrete learner?

4   UDL enables learners to "show their genius" (Fritzgerald, 2020; Posey & Novak, 2020). If the answer to the above question was no, then we as educators are not giving our learners the opportunity to show us what they really know and are capable of doing. UDL is about presuming competence in all of our learners and ensuring that there are ways for every learner to communicate their knowledge and understanding and to showcase their skills. Intentional choices in our lesson design that facilitates this also helps us to know what supports and challenges our learners need to progress this learning, and to identify potential barriers in the next steps and make necessary adjustments.

5   UDL informs, and is informed by, other approaches to equity, diversity, inclusion, and justice. For me, it is the umbrella framework that can include, support, and be supported by other equity focused approaches. I was at a conference once where attendees asked, "why UDL and not cultural responsiveness, or restorative practices, or trauma-informed approaches?" The speaker said if you are doing UDL right, then you are, de-facto, doing the others. I believe there needs to be an awareness and understanding of every approach and one may warrant more attention than another depending on context. However, there is an obvious intersectionality between these approaches that work towards equity, diversity, inclusion, and justice for every learner in our system. We need to recognise that equal potential and equal access hold little value in an unequal world. UDL was designed with this in mind. It was designed to reduce inequities, rather than perpetuate equality (Chardin & Novak, 2020). Fritzgerald (2020) approached this from an honour perspective. Honour our learners' history, their race, religion, culture, social background, etc., and instead of approaching teaching and learning from a power perspective, embrace a code of honour in our classrooms. Chardin and Novak (2020) connect UDL and social justice. These authors show that cultural responsiveness, restorative practices, and

trauma-informed approaches are mindsets that fit with UDL, and vice versa – to reach, support, and challenge our learners who are marginalised by the system and who are traditionally thought about in terms of "something different for" rather than "choice and flexibility within the lesson" when we plan our learning experiences.

6   As educators, we always strive to do our best for our learners and look for new concepts and approaches that will help us achieve that. UDL strives for us to enable our learners to show us their best and truest self, and all of their genius in whatever form that comes. Like everything else, UDL needs to be critiqued, reviewed, and adjusted. CAST are in the process of updating the UDL Guidelines as part of their "UDL Rising to Equity" initiative (CAST, 2021). If we all challenge ourselves to realise equity, to design for variability, remove the barriers to learning, clarify the goals, and enable our learners to show their genius, then our learners will care and be engaged. We and our learners will know how they can build their understanding and develop their skills to achieve their goals. Our learners will know that there is choice and flexibility in how they can engage and communicate their understanding, knowledge, and skills, and what options work best for them in different contexts. This is the potential of UDL.

Belonging and Connecting with Our World of Learning

A core strength of the UDL approach is that it can help create "belonging" and "emotional connection" from the very beginning of your work.

The CAST model of Universal Design for Learning is underpinned by both a philosophy and a practice that recognises there is a great diversity amongst the learners we engage with, and that each and every learner is different. Importantly, the word "universal" does not serve to mean that there is only one optimal solution for every learner – rather, it indicates an awareness of the unique nature of each learner and the need to accommodate differences, creating learning experiences that meet the needs of the learner, and maximise their ability to progress (Rose & Meyer, 2002).

It is worth repeating that the CAST framework does not set out to present one optimal solution for every learner. Rather it embraces the unique nature of each learner together with the need to engage with difference, creating learning experiences to meet the needs of the learner – environments where all learners can continuously realise their true potential (Rose & Meyer, 2002).

Naturally Workable

The CAST model is exceptionally practical due to its focus on planning the learning environment by developing an understanding of all the potential differences, so as to be inclusive of all learners in an increasingly more unifying and less stigmatising way (Rose & Meyer, 2006). While UDL asks that inclusive learning environments be designed from the "get-go", it never negates the need for add-on supports – be it the need of the learner or the need of a group of learners. Learners' needs may, in some instances, be better served with a grouped rather than individualised supports/reasonable accommodations – taking the idea that what works for one may work for many and in fact improve the learning environment.

It is important to remember that UDL emerged from the social model of disability – an approach that appreciates that how society plans and operates may cause barriers, rather than the individual being viewed as a problem that needs to be fixed (i.e., the medical model).

Conclusion

Having had its origins in the fields of architecture and product design, Universal Design has a very clear philosophy – to design environments that are not only usable to the greatest extent possible, regardless of age, ability, or status in life – but moreover an inclusive environment that is aesthetically pleasing and attractive for everyone. By extension, UDL has embraced these principles for the learning environment – and continuously seeks to develop their innovative and inspiring application.

For many, the application is considered in relation to just the tangible curriculum and assessment tools, but the core philosophy of UDL is to create a learning environment that is appealing and attractive for all – and what is more appealing than a learning environment that recognises potential and acknowledges success. This will demand a change of hearts and minds of all engaged in learning as it asks us to reconsider what we mean by engagement and what success looks like.

Traditionally, learning environments have been designed to be competitive – in fact, higher education was designed to be competitive, elite, and exclusive. For many, the idea of being the "best" means working hard, competing aggressively with your peers, while taking criticism and avoiding failure at all costs – what could be a more challenging mindset within which to design a democratic, empowering, and inclusive learning environment?

A designs process seeks to consider all users from the beginning, with an empathetic and considered mindset, while also reviewing and re-evaluating needs and desires as it develops. Consider the simple phone – once designed to make a voice call from one person to another – something not for everyone.

Today the phone is a more than just a "voice calling device" – it is a means for communicating via voice, image, email, enabling reading, learning and even amusement! And most people – young and old – can aspire to own one if they wish! The simple phone is so much more than what it set out to be as it is continuously redesigns for its user. But we can each still choose a phone type that we believe best suits our needs. And there are many types – each designed with a different user in mind.

With the understanding that we are redesigning an environment where "inclusion is everyone's business" (McCarthy, Quirke, & Mc Guckin, 2019), we encourage you to consider what you need to think about more as you develop and implement UDL across the higher education system. It is so much more than applying a framework to some elements of your work. It is our hope that by illuminating what we feel contributes to the development of a Universal Design for Learning inclusionary mindset from inception, we have empowered you to "redesign" and apply such thinking across all aspects of higher education learning. Designing for the diversity of learners and colleagues (not just the academics) who work across the higher education environment is much more than a simplistic view of especially supporting those with a disability, and requires consideration for the wide range of learners who represent the contemporary learning organisation. It also necessitates a greater resilience as there is much to change. However, a UDL approach recognises that we are all potential expert learners and as such offers a unique opportunity where everyone can fully demonstrate their own learning while also contributing to more sustainable approaches in personal and professional development for the new world we face.

Points to Consider

- Which parts of the CAST UDL model are most applicable for your work in higher education?
- What would need to change to enable you to start implementing UDL Guidelines?
- Are there specific aspects of your work that could be easily changed to accommodate variability amongst learners?
- Considering positive participation and potential barriers to engagement in learning activities, what do you think might help learners?
- As you define your role and reframe your thinking, what aspects of the CAST UDL guidelines do you need to reflect further on?

References

Arduini, G. (2020). Curriculum innovation with Universal Design for Learning. *Education Sciences & Society – Open Access, 11*(1), 90–103. Retrieved from: https://ojs.francoangeli.it/_ojs/index.php/ess/article/view/9460. https://doi.org/10.3280/ess1-2020oa9460

Capp, M. J. (2017). The effectiveness of Universal Design for Learning: A meta-analysis of literature between 2013 and 2016. *International Journal of Inclusive Education*, *21*(8), 791–807. https://doi.org/10.1080/13603116.2017.1325074

CAST. (2018). *Universal Design for Learning Guidelines version 2.2.* Retrieved from: http://udlguidelines.cast.org

CAST. (2021). *UDL rising to equity initiative.* Retrieved from: https://www.cast.org/news/2021/udl-rising-equity-advisory-board

Chardin, M., & Novak, K. (2020). *Equity by design: Delivering on the power and promise of UDL.* Thousand Oaks, CA: Corwin Press.

Flood, M., & Banks, J. (2021). Universal Design for Learning: Is it gaining momentum in Irish education?. *Education Sciences*, *11*(7), 341. https://doi.org/10.3390/educsci11070341

Fritzgerald, A. (2020). *Antiracism and Universal Design for Learning: Building expressways to success.* Wakefield, MA: CAST, Incorporated.

Hartmann, E. (2015). Universal design for learning (UDL) and learners with severe support needs. *International Journal of Whole Schooling*, *11*(1), 54–67.

Heelan, A., & Tobin, T. (2021). *UDL for FET practitioners. Guidance for implementing universal design for learning in Irish further education and training.* Dublin, IE: SOLAS & AHEAD Ireland. Retrieved from: https://www.solas.ie/f/70398/x/81044b80ce/fet_practitioners-main.pdf

McCarthy, P., Quirke, M., & Mc Guckin, C. (2019). UDL – *Can you see what I see ... is it an exclusive model or an inclusive model?* Third Pan-Canadian Conference on Universal Design for Learning: Connecting the Dots – Sharing Promising Practices across Country, 2nd–4th October, 2019, Royal Roads University, Victoria, Canada. Abstracts not published.

Meyer, A., Rose, D. H., & Gordon, D. (2014). *Universal Design for Learning: Theory and practice.* Boston, MA: CAST Professional Publishing.

Posey, A., & Novak, K. (2020). *Unlearning: Changing your beliefs and your classroom with UDL.* Wakefield, MA: CAST Publishing.

Rose, D. H., & Meyer, A. (2002). *Teaching every student in the digital age: Universal design for learning.* Association for Supervision and Curriculum Development, 1703 N. Beauregard St., Alexandria, VA 22311-1714 (Product no. 101042).

Rose, D. H., & Meyer, A. (Eds.). (2006). *A practical reader in Universal Design for Learning.* Cambridge, MA: Harvard Education Press.

Rose, T. (2016). *The end of average.* New York: HarperCollins.

Chapter 5

Universal Design in Higher Education

The Experience to Date

Higher education institutions who adopt UD and UDL practices are signalling their awareness of the need for active and meaningful inclusion on their campuses. Our learners from these institutions will become the organisational managers and leaders of the future. If we provide them with direct experience of feeling included, then they will likely reflect upon this experience when they are shaping organisational policies and practices. By modelling active inclusion practices, our institutions are "paying it forwards" and contributing to broader positive social change.

For the most part, UDL actions have really only been evident in activities related to teaching, learning, and assessment. As noted, we need to widen this thinking and application of UD and UDL to all activities on and off campus. Most of our institutions have experience of how this can be operationalised. Inclusive practices have been evident in higher education for quite a while, largely related to the increasing numbers of learners with disabilities enrolling for our courses. Historically, inclusion activities for these learners were the remit of colleagues in the Disability Office or the Access Office. However, what was perhaps once a niche area of activity for institutions – supporting learners with a disability – is now much more central to the operation of all aspects of the institution. For example, the participation rate for learners with disabilities in Irish higher education institutions for the academic year 2020/2021 was nearly 7% – a figure that has been on an annual upward trajectory. Since 2008/2009, Ireland has seen an increase of 269% in the number of learners engaging with Disability Services (AHEAD, 2022).

For this chapter, we focus on the role of the Disability Officer, a professional who has uniquely contributed to the future UDL campus. We explore their role in terms of what they do to assist learners who have a disability, and what they contribute to wider discourse regarding inclusion in our institutions. We argue that the role of the Disability Officer is changing. The change reflects a move from group and personal supports for only those learners who have a disability, to supporting the diversity that is found across our learner population, and the

DOI: 10.4324/9781003137672-6

difficulties that each and every learner might encounter on their learning and experiential journey through higher education. As inclusion experts, Disability Officers are well placed to advise and lead on UDL initiatives. To exemplify our work, we are very grateful to our wonderful colleague Dr John Harding for his case example and reflections on how the University of Cambridge (England) developed from a focus on reasonable adjustments to a more affirmative approach to inclusive teaching and learning.

The Disability Officer

A recurring theme in the literature is the importance for everyone to approach their UD/UDL work "with intent". To fully appreciate this philosophy, we only have to look at the role and work of the Disability Officer. In this chapter, we focus on the work of the Disability Officer, a professional who has uniquely contributed to the future UDL campus.

The Disability Officer is a designated professional who acts as an advocate and facilitator for both the institution and the learner with a disability. The role, whilst in the most part an administrative role, has been the main driver to ensuring inclusion for a learner with a disability. Whilst the core aspect of the role has traditionally been related to conducting needs assessments and organising reasonable accommodations, a more fundamental aspect of the role has been to promote wider inclusionary practices across campus. This widening of the role has reflected the fact that these learners participate in all activities associated with the higher education experience – not just those related to course participation – for example, work placements, clubs and societies, and travel. The niche aspect of the role has become much more central to the operation of the institution as colleagues in other service areas (e.g., library, sports, careers) have recognised the need to consult with the Disability Officer to adjust their services for these learners. Over time, the recognition developed that a more pragmatic approach would be to pre-empt any exclusionary practices with a UD/UDL approach capable of promoting an active inclusion agenda across campus. Importantly, such thinking has resulted in policies and practices that have been inclusive of all learners – not just those within the remit of the Disability Officer. As the role of the Disability Officer continues to evolve, their expertise and knowledge plays a central role in how UD/UDL thinking and practices will allow for greater flexibility – and success – in our work.

Learners need support in all aspects of learning including academic, emotional, and social demands when engaging in higher education. Offering this designated support to learners with a disability contributes to a higher quality of education and greater opportunities for success. Where inclusive practices were evident prior to the advent of a UD approach, the Disability Service was often seen as part of the wider student/learner support services, primarily located within the student support services. As UD becomes a shared responsibility this might change, and so might the role of the Disability Officer.

The History of the Disability Service on Campus

When learners with disabilities began to engage in higher education in greater numbers, they were primarily directed to a designated individual, often known as the Disability Officer or the Access Officer. This individual was charged with the administrative responsibility of ensuring that the needs of the learner were met. For the most part, these needs were often focused on gaining access to the basic requirements needed to engage with learning tasks – for example, the ability to access books, reading materials, lecture notes, and orientation. The physical location of where the learning was taking place was also a factor, even if it meant that the learner could only attend a lecture if it meant sitting at the back of the auditorium. Until relatively recently, there was not much available in terms of technology to support access, and it was often a challenge for academics to embrace some of the recommendations made for these learners (e.g., audio recording of lectures). Such approaches were haphazard and represented an after-the-fact add-on approach that could be considered as being "special" rather than "reasonable" in terms of accommodating the needs of the learner.

Reasonable Accommodation

The idea of an accommodation being "reasonable" came later, often enshrined in legislation. In the learning environment, a reasonable accommodation represents a change to practice that has the intention of ensuring that a learner with a disability can engage effectively with the curriculum and the environment they find themselves in. Reasonable accommodations are intended to ensure that a disability does not prohibit participation and is a legislative responsibility when a learner discloses that they have a recognised disability. The important point here is that the accommodation (e.g., extra time for an examination, assistive technology) should not confer an advantage to the learner. Rather, the accommodation should be designed in a manner that enables the learner to participate on an equal basis with their non-disabled peers. If the accommodation does provide an advantage, then it is neither fair nor reasonable.

While the legislative imperative served to copper-fasten the role of the Disability Officer, it also presented an opportunity to develop activities and resources that improved the wider educational experience of learners. The success of this work is evidenced in the increasing requests that are received from learners without a disability seeking improvements and accommodations that could enhance their own learning experience. This bottom-up approach has acted as a significant driver for wider inclusion initiatives across our institutions. Rather than simply being about teaching, learning, and assessment related issues, the focus has widened to improve not just access but participation, experience, and belonging.

From Reasonable Accommodations to Inclusion for All

Success in relation to inclusion and disability has often been measured and determined by the number of learners with a disability accessing courses, rather than by the number who successfully complete their studies. This emphasis, while well intentioned, continued to support a separatist approach. The Disability Officer's role has continually developed over the years as they advocate for successful learning experiences for learners with a disability across the different faculties and services on campus. They have developed significant working relationships with many services (e.g., library, sports). Whilst it might now seem strange to think of having individuals read for learners with a text disability, there was a time in our recent past where this was not at all unusual. Supports such as this, provided with the greatest of intentions, were often disabling, having arisen from a medical model perspective. The focus to consider the disability and recommend an add-on to ensure access was proving to be disabling in and of itself.

What is noteworthy has been the emancipatory approach of those individuals engaged with Disability Services. Over the years, as they embraced assistive technologies and promoted greater independence in learning, they recognised the disabling effects of simply providing add-on supports. Two issues arose and served to focus the mind. Firstly, learners were becoming dependant on other people for their participation efforts. Secondly, the increasing numbers of learners with a disability entering higher education did not come with a concomitant rise in funding available to support the needs of these learners. A solution was required that could empower the learner to become more independent and take on more responsibility for their own learning experience.

A New Approach to Inclusion

The continuing rise in participation rates for learners with a disability, and similar increases in the general diversity of the learner population, required new thinking and approaches to inclusion in higher education. The once effective method of designating responsibly for "inclusive practice" to one or a limited number of professionals was no longer effective. What became needed was a new way to offer support and active inclusion initiatives that could be targeted at all learners, albeit with a recognition that there would always be some learners who would need access to individualised supports that could be provided through the role of the Disability Officer.

The philosophy and practices associated with UD and UDL provided fresh and contemporary thinking about how to include, the greatest extent possible, from the get-go. A UD/UDL approach offered an opportunity to rethink the institution approach to inclusion, encouraging a move towards a model of shared responsibility. Just as the "design to include" approach worked for architecture, it was becoming evident that this also worked for education. Whilst the initial focus and evidence was understood from a school-based perspective, there was increasing evidence from colleges in the US that a UD/UDL approach could be successful and could be applied to higher education too.

This approach made intuitive sense. Provision of the same supports worked for so many learners because they improved the learning and participation experience and brought about a degree of flexibility to learning that had not been seen before. Where once traditional, hierarchical, and the "silo thinking" expert approach was appreciated, UD/UDL presented a novel and interesting challenge to embrace and develop a truly inter- and multi-disciplinary inclusive community approach.

Applications of UDL have been successful and have highlighted that individualised add-ons are only required for some learners. As campus communities enacted small changes in their approaches to active inclusion, the feeling and experience of difference was felt less, and the community of learners experiencing positive learning experiences grew. We only have to consider our recent experience with Covid-19 to recognise that such changes to practice – sometimes subtle and sometimes radical – have presented novel and beneficial effects for all of us. For example, technology adaption and flexibility in working hours and location have made us all realise that some work practices that seemed "set in stone" could, and probably should, be changed – giving us all flexibility and choice. For many of us, these changes have brought about other flexibilities and positive changes in our daily and family lives.

Despite obvious opportunities, a legacy prevails in terms of the "expert approach". We need to remain cautious and vigilant, remembering that inclusive thinking and practice is far from achieved in higher education. For some, disability is still understood and "managed" in a separatist approach. The notion that all roads point to the Disability Officer when there is an issue prevails, with the challenge being to appreciate that inclusive practice is about continuous change. Such change must be at both the personal and the structural levels. Redesigning approaches to our work in higher education requires thinking not just about the learner of today but also about the learner of the future.

The Disability Officer: A Key Consultant and Advocate for UDL

Up to this point, we have made specific reference to the role of the Disability Officer. However, we recognise that this professional role might not exist in every higher education institution. But, as the world shifts from a medical to a social model of thinking and now to one of UD, most higher education institutions have a designated person with an expertise in disability-related issues. Whilst titles and role definitions might differ (e.g., Access Officer,

Rehabilitative Officer), someone has to assume responsibility for the organisation of reasonable accommodations. We find this to be the case across both public and private higher education.

Innovative inclusion practices over recent times have been supported, if not driven, by significant national and international policy initiatives. The combination of these, together with the developing interest of learner support staff, has shifted inclusive thinking towards a model of UD and its approach to learning. In the past, inclusion was framed predominantly by the need to abide by legislation, together with an emerging agenda from the UNCRPD, with the Disability Officer being best placed to make proactive, as well as reactive, change. UD is about attitude, ethos, and an appreciation of what it takes to be inclusive – across the whole higher education community. Inclusion is no longer the job of just one professional. While the professional who has lobbied for inclusion for those with a disability has a key role on the future UD campus, as we keep reminding colleagues, inclusion is everyone's business.

The Disability Officer has a wealth of experience, including the key competencies required to advise on the development and implementation of new approaches in an environment that is everchanging. The Disability Officer is a skilled advocate for change who has access to, and the trust of, both the learner and senior management. They engage at the most senior levels on campus and have mediated where there have been challenges in the past. Most importantly, they have a unique view of what active inclusion really means in a practical way.

It is understandable that a Disability Officer can become frustrated when every problem that seems to be related to disability lands at their door – often unnecessarily. This frustration can be exasperated when the same problems keep coming to their door, due to a lack of appreciation of what some simple changes to our work practices can result in for the learner. They are skilled at seeing beyond individual solutions and can quickly recognise system changes that can take place and be beneficial for all learners. Moreover, they can support colleagues to make the necessary changes – even if they do not fully understand what it is they have to do. Disability Officers have traditionally been seen as the solution, when in fact the solution is to change how we do things that continue to exclude the learner. This new approach will never negate the need for add-on supports for some learners.

Moving Inclusion Across the Campus: Beyond Disability

Policy and practice regarding active inclusion has been gathering momentum across all levels of education. Notably, much of our knowledge about the success of a UDL approach has been gleaned from applications in post-primary education settings. The focus of UDL implementation in the other levels of education has been predominantly on teacher development and revisions to pedagogical practices. On the higher education campus, this innovative approach is being increasingly adopted, in the main, by an agenda that seeks more meaningful inclusion for the diversity of learners that we see on campus today. Higher education is more complex and nuanced than the school sector, and with its ability to be applied to much more than teaching, learning, and assessment activities, UDL can be beneficial to everyone's work in higher education.

Whilst some people might argue that disability should be treated as a separate entity to the "equality, diversity, and inclusion" initiatives that we increasingly see in our institutions, we see this as a fundamental challenge for colleagues – at a personal and systemic level. There is an increasing need to recognise that disability and inclusion are part of the wider diversity debate, while not losing sight of the fact that learners with disabilities may, in certain circumstances, continue to require specific supports. It is important to recognise that whilst disability services were originally framed by a medical model approach (e.g., prescribing accommodations), Disability Officers are amongst the greatest advocates for new ways of thinking about inclusion and inclusive practices within higher education. One thing is for sure, and we have all witnessed this through the Covid-19 pandemic, that the future of learning in our institutions will see continuous and evolving change. These developments will not just be focused on our learners with disabilities – they will be for each and every learner and colleague. We have moved quite a bit from the original emphasis on securing access and participation in the lecture hall. Our shared future in higher education needs to frame active inclusion in terms of not just equality but belonging and shared responsibility.

A UDL ecosystem can allow everyone in the institution to feel that they have a valuable contribution to make to this new way of thinking. That is why there is a need to recognise that on the contemporary campus inclusion is no longer just the business of the Disability Officer. Rather, it is everyone's business. This does not mean that someone should not take the lead, but it might require a change in institutional culture. The person who might be best equipped to lead on such work is the Disability Officer.

Current Challenges: Sharing the Culture of Inclusion

As noted above, embracing a UDL approach to inclusion necessitates a shared approach. A widespread implementation of a UDL philosophy and practice in higher education will support the diversity that exists among our learner population, as well as the similar diversity that exists among ourselves and our colleagues. By its very nature, UDL will evidence a reduction in the need for reasonable accommodations and other costly add-ons to the work that we do.

This will require change for everyone, including the Disability Officer. An interesting point for consideration is whether this will mean a change of job title or role. Perhaps there might be a more fundamental reconceptualisation of the role – to that of a "Universal Design Officer" who has a special interest in reasonable accommodations. As well as the possibility of a changing role for the Disability Officer, other colleagues, including teaching and learning staff, will need to adopt and adapt too. Perhaps the most conservative of colleagues and lecturing staff in terms of change would really need to embrace UDL. This can be difficult for a few reasons. For example, many of our teaching colleagues do not possess a teaching qualification or foundational knowledge in pedagogical practices and knowledge of how learners learn, teaching methodologies, and differentiation. Also, the lecturer is traditional viewed as the doyen of all knowledge in their specialist area and expert in how to impart this knowledge to learners. Whilst academic freedom is to be cherished, it should not be used as a defence to being reflexive and considering if the approach to teaching could be enhanced. An easy approach for the lecturer is to trial Behling and Tobin's (2018) "plus one" approach.

A simple analogy is to consider recycling. In our moves to embrace environment-friendly practices, we all have access to bins on campus for separate forms of waste. It is no longer one person's job to separate the waste. Where once we were unsure as to how to approach this new way of discarding our rubbish, or maybe even have had little interest or considered it an unnecessary change, we now embrace the new practice. Similarly with inclusive practice, we need to change our thinking and action. Recycling required a change of attitude and action – at personal and systemic levels. Similarly, a UDL approach does not come by accident. It too needs a change of attitude and action. It is a learned approach that requires mindful and responsive consideration.

To successfully implement UDL in higher education, a multidisciplinary approach is necessary. And this needs to include those with knowledge about active inclusion and how to accommodate learners at both the group and the individual level. Thus, the Disability Officer should be a key member of any team that seeks to introduce UDL to our work (Quirke, McCarthy, Treanor, & Mc Guckin, 2019). Whilst their work has traditionally been restricted to those learners with a disability, a UDL approach might see their work change from "disability" to any learner who has a "difficulty".

This shared responsibility and wider view of inclusion encourages us to take personal responsibility, form new relationships with colleagues, and move away from the expert model. Dialogue must take place. If we all reflect upon and consider the work that we do for our learners, and then have the courage to implement small and incremental adjustments to our work practices, then fairly soon the whole institution will be "designing for inclusion". To get started with this, we would encourage colleagues to develop or join a Community of Practice (CoP). There is wonderful guidance and encouragement to be found in the downloadable guidance document for implementing UDL in the Irish Further Education and Training sector, authored by Heelan and Tobin (2021). In Chapter 7, Carrie Archer shares her experience of implementing UDL and the challenges that she and her colleagues faced.

Support Need on the Future Campus: Points to Ponder

The primary driver to "include" and to enable meaningful conversations with those that feel excluded and need to identify support needs is the needs assessment process. There are also many other versions of "needs assessment" to be found in education, primarily in the special education field, including Individual Education Plans and Individual Personnel Plans, with recent take-up in the world of employment. The process is unique to the world of disability – perhaps a legacy from the medical approach while it was also a very useful tool in the social world of disability.

Needs assessment is a process whereby the impact of disability is considered in terms of identifying supports and accommodations, together with the individual impacted. Primarily a face-to-face administrative function, it has developed over the years in terms of practice, ethos, and value. It allows for a genuine dialogue to take place about the impact of disability and has led to a greater understanding of the unnecessary challenges faced by people with disabilities. While it can be argued that it has its origins in medical and caring professions as a "diagnostic tool" for people with disabilities, it has its merits and cannot be dismissed – even in a contemporary Universal Design world.

It, in essence, ensures that the need for add-on supports is not denied in a new inclusive world. However, what needs to be considered currently – and has been given little thought – is where this process that has stood the test of time fits in the new ecosystem that Universal Design demands, most particularly in a higher education learning environment. This section will set out some consideration worthy of exploration as the higher education campus redesigns its approaches for a culture and practice of inclusion.

- The first consideration is that needs assessment requires a multidisciplinary approach. Interestingly, this is something that it shares with a Universal Design Approach – as good design demands that the primary needs of the clients are met in collaboration with all users. What perhaps needs to be reconsidered is who should be involved. It is often argued that the learner should be the driver – and yes that is true. But while the learner is most familiar with their disability and its demands, they are not an expert on curriculum or the world of higher education. Therefore, perhaps a shift needs to occur where a greater collaboration of more than just the disability service and the learner needs to take place (McCarthy, Quirke & Treanor, 2018). For inclusion to be everyone's business, there is a need for others to take up a position in this relationship while using the expertise of the disability service when needed.
- A second consideration is about how grouped and individual supports are considered. When deliberating the approach to grouped or individual support as outlined in the Inclusion Triangle, supports are sometimes overlooked as the emphasis is on the design of the shared environment.

How grouped and individual supports are designed around need and implemented requires a consistent approach and shared understanding if quality and ethical standards are to be met and an ad-hoc approach avoided.

- A third consideration is about the conversation to include. The language, terminology, and tone of conversation around inclusion will have to be reconsidered. Increasingly, people do not want their disability or difference to define them – they wish to have a more positive conversation about what they need to achieve. The language of disability is one of the past, and while it is necessary to appreciate disability as part of one's identity, it is unnecessary to continue to apply a deficit model of thinking. Social justice demands that we change not just the language but also the terminology and tone of conversation around inclusion. We must appreciate those we are seeking to work with and recognise the damage of labels and definitions. Disclosure is a key part of this discourse – how someone discusses their disability and the needs around it are very individual and this conversation can change depending on so many factors. Disability Services on campus have done a lot of work on this over the years, resulting in a higher profile for supports and less stigma being attached to many. What was once seen as an embarrassment is now coveted by many learners (access to audio books, for example). However, there are still many areas of disability that are difficult and a lot of bias prevails. As there will always be a situation where an accommodation would be required, it is necessary that we continue to support learners sensitively and not see Universal Design as a means to cutting resources.
- A fourth consideration is the need to respect inclusion as it moves beyond the lecture hall and classroom. Universal Design practices and thinking have also to be applied to work placements, Erasmus experiences, college social experiences, library access, etc. Learners no longer attend college just to learn the curriculum – they want the experience of campus. And moreover, employers appreciate it when they have made the most of their time in college. No learner can be left out or excluded from so many areas of college life that are considered the norm by others. This necessitates the needs assessment to perhaps consider all aspects of college life.
- A fifth and final consideration (for now!) is that supports and design environment must be defined by "need" more so than disability – this is not without its challenge. All learners need to feel that they can access, participate, and feel like they belong in all aspects of college life – even if they choose not to participate. And this will require shifting the "needs assessment" to one that is more about aspirations and hopes. It is such thinking that might redesign what is a reactive process to one of ambassador – negotiating a path when there prove to be challenges. This would mean that staff and other members of the campus community could also avail of such a service when they feel that their approaches need to be "redesigned".

Reasonable Accommodations for the Future

It has often been surmised that on the future Universal Design campus the disability officer will be out of a job. But when we consider the need to ensure a sustainable approach to inclusion framed by a positive attitude to the changes that Universal Design and its approaches in higher education demand, together with the evolution of Reasonable Accommodations, this is perhaps the furthest thing from the truth! It is perhaps true the emphasis will shift in terms of who will be able to avail of the knowledge and support – and how the supports and know-how will be shared.

There are many challenges for future learning and when we stop and consider all the changes that have taken place in recent years, many of the challenges have been for the staff that support the learners in all aspects of their teaching and learning. Having to come to grips with new information technology – now almost on a daily basis – is not without its frustrations. And when we stop and consider advances in

> virtual reality, and new course design, (whether it incorporates flexible, blended eLearning, social media approaches or not), together with the new diversity of learners that continue to engage and with high expectations of the college environment – we may need to reconsider and recognise the "new excluded" – the academic!

Such changes in learning will also demand change in what reasonable accommodations are and look like. As accommodations are identified, there will be a need to be pragmatic in engaging with both faculty and learners so as to pre-empt any exclusionary practices. Learners can become cocreators of the new Universal Design campus but need to have the skills to do so. Do we need to understand all things technological in our classrooms? Are we ready to reconsider what is fair and equal in learning and assessment? Can we truly identify what are exclusionary entry criteria and practices on courses – particularly professional courses?

Thinking "Universal Design" can be used to assess our practices and with learner support services explore what is fair and equitable for all learners if we are to promote a greater agenda of inclusion across the new campus of learning. It is this thinking that will ensure that every learner is engaged in learning – in a just way.

Case Example: From Reasonable Adjustment to UDL – Developing Conceptions of Support Models for Disabled Learner/Students in Higher Education

John Harding from the University of Cambridge, England, presents us with a useful and thoughtful case example and reflection on how the thoughts and ideas in this chapter can be enacted in a higher education institution.

John Harding

I have been the Head of the Disability Resource Centre (DRC), the support service for disabled students at the University of Cambridge, England, since 2008. The University of Cambridge is a research-intensive higher education institution with a long-held reputation for academic excellence. Cambridge is a globally diverse institution with students from over 147 different countries. It can be a place of great innovation, but at times, given its traditions and culture, it can also approach change with caution.

Since starting in 2008, the proportion of disabled students within the total student population at Cambridge has increased from under 4% to nearly 17%. In 2008 we had approximately 600 disabled students. Thirteen years later in 2021, we have nearly 4,100 (total student population of 24,250). Similar increases have been seen across all UK universities.

Essentially, this is a positive phenomenon, and suggests that widening participation initiatives and protections for disabled people has increased their participation in higher education. It has also brought to the forefront debates about how best equitable access to education can be secured for this cohort of students.

In the last five years or more there has also been some significant movement in the way in which the development of models of support for disabled students have been framed. In part, this has been driven by the increase in numbers but also by the discourse around inclusive education, developing conceptual models of disability and specifically around the theory of UDL.

For example, in 2017 the UK's Department for Education (DfE) issued a guidance document entitled "Inclusive Teaching and Learning in Higher Education as a route to Excellence". This guidance references both the social model of disability, which argues that disability is a societal construct, not situated with the individual (Oliver, 1983), and the affirmative model of disability, which seeks to normalise disability (Cameron, 2010, 2011, 2014; Swain & French, 2000). It is worth noting that, by citing the affirmative model of disability for the first time in an official government document, the guidance encourages a move beyond the current individualistic orthodoxy in models of disabled student support – what Liasidou calls "deficit-oriented" perspectives (2014). It promotes a universal design approach where disability and impairment are normalised (or de-problematised) and differences are accepted and calls for these principles to be demonstrated in the design and development of educational policy and practice – in effect, adopting a UDL approach. It is also important to note that this focus is not only specifically aimed at disabled students; it applies to students with a range of protected characteristics (e.g., race, gender). In fact, it applies to all students. This official shift in philosophical position is of great significance to those working at the coalface of disability support in tertiary education.

In order to understand this significance it is worthwhile to briefly detail the history of the legislative underpinning of disability support services. The UK's Disability Discrimination Act (DDA) of 1995 introduced the concept of "reasonable adjustments". This represented an active approach that required service providers and employers to identify and remove barriers to participation for disabled people. This was followed by the establishment of legal rights for disabled students in higher education through the Special Educational Needs and Disability Act (SENDA) in 2001. In 2010 the DDA was replaced by the Equality Act, which strengthened provisions for disabled people in higher education. In the period following the extension of the DDA in 2005 there was a steep increase in the participation of disabled students in higher education, many of whom were supported by the public funds available through Disabled Students' Allowances (DSAs). Arguably, this steep increase and the concomitant demand on DSAs funding acted as a key stimulus for the government to review models of support for disabled students in higher education (i.e., more than its philosophical commitment to the social or affirmative models).

These increases in participation have, however, stretched the existing mechanisms for support, which were designed for individual adjustments for far fewer students, to the point where they are no longer sustainable, threatening institutions' abilities to meet their statutory duties in this regard.

> ...research concluded that universities should place more emphasis on developing inclusive curricula, incorporating principles of universal design. This would obviate the need to certify students as disabled, ... and would remove the need for lecturers to make numerous ad hoc adjustments. Some students, however, would continue to need very specific and individualised adjustments.
>
> (Fuller et al., 2009, p. 28)

However, despite this developing emphasis on inclusive practice, some (Ahmed 2012; Gibson, 2015) argue that in reality very little has yet changed, with disabled students mostly shoe-horned into established models of support and teaching.

Inclusive policy, as it was and is, endeavours to relocate disabled students into mainstream systems, and therefore "...a misunderstood and misrepresented form of 'inclusion' is practised in education. 'Inclusion' becomes about attempts to induct that which is 'different' into already established forms and dominant institutional cultures" (Gibson, 2015, p. 878).

For Gibson, the drive towards inclusive education has "failed". She argues that what is needed is a "...post-rights inclusive pedagogy", moving away from a medicalised model which sees disability as pathology and "...as something to be normalised via the application of particular teaching methods or technologies ..." (2015, p. 882), a position which clearly supports the application of the principles of UDL and an affirmative model of disability approach.

The affirmative model stresses the importance of valuing people for who they are rather than focussing on what they are not. Cameron posits that the affirmative model is

> a tool to be used by practitioners working alongside disabled people in examining their own roles in sustaining or challenging disabling expectations and relationships, and in working as allies who have a role in transforming the structures and institutions by which all our lives are shaped.
>
> (2011, p. 22)

Understanding this relatively new conception of disability can inform strategic thinking on provision of support for disabled students in higher education. In many ways disability services find themselves caught between their own affirmative philosophical positions and the need to facilitate support via national and institutional systems and processes that have a medical/deficit model design. In order to access funding and support, students in the UK HE sector have to present *evidence*, have to prove they fall under the legal definition of disability, have to *disclose their disability* (note – not their impairment). The relevance of this discussion lies in the need to find efficient and effective solutions for the current concerns around institutions meeting their legal duties to disabled students – solutions that are universally beneficial rather than focusing on one sub-group and which rely less on, or indeed remove, the need for labelling, for disclosure, for "evidence", and for "othering" (Martin, 2012).

This question of identity and labelling/othering is played out in the feedback we receive from disabled students at Cambridge, a large proportion of whom do not identify as disabled people even though they are aware that they fall under the legal definition of disability. It also aligns with the principles of UDL which seek to provide multiple means of engagement, representation, and action and expression, removing the need for separate or "special" treatment. This is important when considering and evaluating interventions (such as providing recordings of lectures) which in many ways remove the need for disclosure and labelling and offer a single and equitable point of access which does not emphasise deficit but does cater for difference. This recognition of the ubiquity of difference is a central tenet of the affirmative model of disability and UDL.

It is my view that the drive towards more inclusive teaching and learning practices and a greater emphasis on the affirmative model, or just seeing all students as having a range of differing access require-ments, will start to lead to the *evidence* and the *diagnosis* being less important. Also, as institutions take on more responsibility for developing their own internal inclusive practices, they rely far less on external funding mechanisms (such as DSAs) which employ a medical model approach, aiding the shift to a more universal and affirmative approach. The development by the University of Cambridge of their own internal Reasonable Adjustments Fund (RAF) was used as a case study as an example of such a strategic and inclusive approach within the Department for Education's 2017 DfE Guidance on inclusive practice.

Enhanced legal provisions and developing conceptions of disability have had a positive impact on the participation of disabled people in higher education, particularly in the last decade. Individualised models of support become unsustainable once disabled student numbers reflect the true prevalence of disability within the general population. Therefore, approaches which seek to normalise disability are now required and are supported by the promotion of UDL and by govern-mental demands for demonstration of inclusive practice. This need for change has influenced the adoption of new pedagogical and technological practices and in addressing the disadvantage many disabled students face.

In response to these external and internal drivers, and to the concerns that models of support were not truly inclusive, or logistically viable, in June 2017, the Disability Resource Centre submitted a paper to the University of Cambridge's General Board's Education Committee detailing nine recommendations to develop policy and practice in relation to inclusive teaching and learning:

1   Further embed inclusive teaching and learning within University strategy and vision;
2   The Cambridge Centre for Teaching and Learning (CCTL) Steering Group coordinate and implement the recommendations resulting from this report (the CCTL works with staff to enrich educational practice, funds innovation, and encourages the exchange of ideas and methods);
3   Promote inclusive teaching and learning case studies via CCTL website;
4   Introduce greater utilisation teaching awards to reward inclusive practice;
5   Increase collaboration between the DRC and academic faculties and departments on development and understanding of inclusive teaching and learning;
6   Further develop collaborative partnerships between librarians and academic staff to support the use of technology and online platforms in teaching and learning;
7   Strengthen recognition of inclusive practice within academic promotion pathways;
8   Support the extension and expansion of the Lecture Capture pilot;
9   Develop inclusive teaching and learning online training modules.

All nine recommendations were approved.

Alongside this, in late 2020, I led a working group (with student representation) to revise our policy in relation to the support of disabled students, incorporating the principles of inclusive/universal design. This policy came into force for the 2021–22 academic year. Previously this was called "Code of Practice: Reasonable Adjustments for Disabled Students" but has been renamed "Code of Practice: Access and Inclusion for Disabled Students". Whilst it does still refer to the legislative framework on which our legal duties to disabled students are based, the emphasis is on applying the principles of UDL to design out many reactive adjustments by making the curriculum, assessment, and the teaching environment (including teaching practice) more inclusive from the outset.

To support these policy changes it is vital that conceptualisations of student disability services are reframed; moving away from a "welfare" or "wellbeing" model, which is situated in a medical/deficit model perspective, to one which is more affirmative and based on the principles of UDL. Disability specialists should work in conjunction with their academic and professional services colleagues to design a more inclusive and accessible teaching and learning environment. There is still a long way to go, but it certainly feels that the momentum is with us, and this can only benefit all students (including disabled students) and the staff who work with them.

This article was, in part, drawn from a revision of the introduction to my Doctorate in Education Registration Report (2018).

A New Beginning...

There is no doubt that the need to shift to a broader concept of inclusion using a Universal Design approach is now being taken seriously. And the greatest advocates of the approach are those who have been dealing with exclusion and a separatist approach for people with disabilities on campus for over two decades now. Whether it is considered by some as a fad or not, what is recognised is that any approach to improve inclusive practice is the right thing to do. Disability Officers together with their colleagues in student/learner support services and allies across the academy have continuously pushed to redesign practices, curriculum, and assessment.

Disability Officers have engaged across the campus and will need to continue to do so if changes are to be made. Change is never easy – and particularly when an audience is steeped in tradition, focused on research and validity, and whose job it is to question efficacy and critically analyse any approach. This is perhaps one of those times that practice will inform theory – whether it is simply due to a moral compass or a greater recognition that sustainable education will have to be redesigned for future learners.

The Disability Officer role and service is evolving and this will have a domino effect. The Disability Officer role on a new inclusive campus will have to change – just as all other roles will change. Perhaps it will become more of a generalist role – as inclusion moves to being a shared way of thinking and acting. Such change is the start of something new…

Points to Consider

- Whose "job" is it to advocate and support inclusive practice in your higher education institution?
- What would a "UDL" strategy look like for your institution, and would some roles have to change?
- What would be the implications for your role?
- Do you have a "voice"? How could you contribute in a meaningful way to developing a UDL agenda on campus?

References

AHEAD. (2022). *Students with disabilities engaged with support services in higher education in Ireland 2020/21.* Dublin, Ireland: AHEAD Educational Press. ISBN: 978-1-8380513-6-5

Ahmed, S. (2012). *On being included. Racism and diversity in institutional life.* New York, NY: Duke University Press.

Behling, K. T., & Tobin, T. J. (2018). *Reach everyone, teach everyone: universal design for learning in higher education.* West Virginia University Press.

Cameron, C. (2010). *Does anybody like being disabled? A critical exploration of impairment, identity, media and everyday experience in a disabling society.* (Unpublished doctoral thesis). Queen Margaret University, Scotland.

Cameron, C. (2011). Not our problem: Impairment as difference, disability as role. *Journal of Inclusive Practice in Further and Higher Education, 3*(2), 10–25.

Cameron, C. (2014). Developing an affirmative model of disability and impairment. In J. Swain, S. French, C. Barnes, & S. Thomas (Eds.), *Disabling barriers – enabling environments* (3rd ed., pp. 24–30). London: Sage.

Fuller, M., Georgeson, J., Healey, M., Hurst, A., Kelly, K., Riddell, S., … & Weedon, E. (2009). *Improving disabled students' learning.* London and New York: Routledge.

Gibson, S. (2015). When rights are not enough: What is? Moving towards new pedagogy for inclusive education within UK universities. *International Journal of Inclusive Education, 19*(8), 875–886. https://doi.org/10.1080/13603116.2015.1015177

Heelan, A., & Tobin, T. (2021). *UDL for FET practitioners. Guidance for implementing universal design for learning in Irish further education and training.* Dublin, IE: SOLAS & AHEAD Ireland. Retrieved from: https://www.solas.ie/f/70398/x/81044b80ce/fet_practitioners-main.pdf

Liasidou, A. (2014). Critical disability studies and socially just change in higher education. *British Journal of Special Education, 41*(2), 120–135. https://doi.org/10.1111/1467-8578.12063

Martin, N. (2012). Disability identity–disability pride. *Perspectives: Policy and Practice in Higher Education, 16*(1), 14–18. https://doi.org/10.1080/1360310 8.2011.611832

McCarthy, P., Quirke, M., & Treanor, D. (2018). *The role of the disability officer and the disability service in higher education in Ireland.* DAWN: Dublin. Available at: https://www.ahead.ie/userfiles/files/shop/free/The%20_Role_of_the_ Disability_Officer.pdf

Oliver, M. (1983). Social work and disability: Old and new directions. In *Social Work with disabled people* (pp. 6–32). Practical Social Work Series. London: Palgrave. https://doi.org/10.1007/978-1-349-86058-6_2

Quirke, M., McCarthy, P., Treanor, D., & Mc Guckin, C. (2019). Tomorrow's disability officer – A cornerstone on the universal design campus. *Journal of Inclusive Practice in Further and Higher Education (JIPFHE), 11*(1), 29–42.

Swain, J., & French, S. (2000). Towards an affirmation model of disability. *Disability & Society, 15*(4), 569–582. https://doi.org/10.1080/0968759005 0058189

Chapter 6

A Campus Where UDL Thinking Is Everyone's Business

The previous chapters have explored how the concepts of UD and UDL have developed from changing social attitudes to people with disabilities. The first step on this journey was the recognition that the medical model, whilst useful and important, also served to exclude. The more inclusive social model of disability resulted in many important changes to legislation which, in turn, had a direct impact upon policies and practices. A key expression of these developments can be seen through the role of the Disability Officer and other active inclusion initiatives on campus. Whilst Disability Officers were early pioneers of UDL, advocating for its ability to create inclusive learning experiences for learners with disabilities, there is now the recognition that these ideas and practices must go beyond disability.

Any examination of the cohort of learners that we meet on campus will demonstrate that higher education is increasingly becoming more representative of the society that we live in – with more learners who have a disability – including intellectual disability, adult and returning learners, learners from economically disadvantaged areas, visiting learners from across the world, and all of the richness and diversity that we experience through the various cultures and religions that our learners represent. Whilst there is some evidence of good practice emerging, with other colleagues adopting approaches to ensure inclusion in novel ways, there is an opportunity for everyone involved in higher education to come together and share a UDL approach. As you read this, you can probably think of an aspect of your own practice where you can show that it is inclusive. The key trick is, however, to ensure that this has been done with intent, and that it was planned from the get-go.

UDL is not confined to disability – it seeks to include in the broadest possible sense. Inclusion is truly everyone's business. UDL is for anyone who has an interest in social justice and the equality of opportunity for each and every learner to reach their full potential. UDL presents a great opportunity for all of

DOI: 10.4324/9781003137672-7

the contemporary work that is being done in relation to "Equality, Diversity, and Inclusion" (EDI) initiatives. In this chapter we make this argument and set out the importance of such inclusionary thinking, and how a broader application of UDL philosophy and practice can be of benefit to all of our learners, to our colleagues, and to our own work. So, this is a chapter for everyone on campus.

The ideas and arguments presented in this chapter are supported by contributions from Dr Cristina Devecchi and Andratesha Fritzgerald. Cristina outlines past theories and how they continue to frame our thinking about inclusion. Active inclusion is at the heart of what we do, and this is particularly exemplified by Andratesha's contribution, where it is evident that UDL can be a potent thinking and action tool for social justice issues that are central to inclusion for many of our learners.

UDL: A Yardstick and Not a Template

Throughout this book we have encouraged you to start your UDL journey with some personal reflection and thought about your own experiences with feeling excluded, and how small changes can lead to a sense of understanding and feeling included. We believe that this is important, because a true UDL approach to our practice is not simply applying or completing a rigid checklist to our work and exhorting to everyone that "I've UDL'd it!". We have mentioned that we have seen this approach too much. Without changing hearts and minds (our own first), a UDL approach will just become the latest fad, and something that we feel that we need to engage with to satisfy a departmental or institutional policy.

Because this is your journey, we want to "show you where to look, but not what to see". UDL can result in many wonderful applications to practice, and for the work that you do for our learners, you are the person best placed to understand how a UDL approach might be beneficial to developing something that is new, innovative, challenging, interesting, and engaging. We can all get stuck in using the same old approaches in our work. We tend to move through each academic year on autopilot. Engaging with UDL might just give each of us some renewed motivation and job satisfaction. For all of these reasons, we encourage you to see your work with UDL as being more akin to a yardstick approach, with estimations and approximations, rather than as a rigid and "tick-the-box" checklist. By their very nature, checklists suggest that there is a definitive end-point. UDL is iterative, never standing still, being reflective and proactive, and all with the goal of increasing the potential of each learner to access their learning and demonstrate their knowledge and understanding. To do this, we have to continuously challenge ourselves and our view of inclusion. As mentioned in the previous chapter about "communities of practice", you could work with a friend or colleague on beginning your UDL work – looking to a "plus one" approach initially, checking whether the approach was useful, making amendments, re-trying, and so on.

Higher Education Campuses: Past, Present, and Future

When we consider who traditionally attended higher education, it is evident that it was the privileged few – primarily male and economically advantaged. We do not have to look back too far in history to see the exclusion of women from the full advantages of higher education. For example, in our own world-renowned university, Trinity College Dublin, it was only in 1904 that degrees could be awarded to women. After the board meeting that approved the decision to award degrees to women, the Provost of the College, George Salmon, is alleged to have said that women would only be admitted to Trinity as learners over his dead body. Coincidentally, Salmon died less than one week after the utterance.

Over our recent history, the elitism of higher education has meant that learners from marginalised groups, including those with disabilities, have clearly been the exception rather than the norm. Representation and inclusion were, therefore, not issues that needed to be understood or addressed. Whilst it could be argued that participation in higher education is still privileged, much has changed and continues to change on our campuses. Consequently, it is timely we have an open and honest dialogue about what we really mean by inclusion and, what an active inclusion agenda for higher education should look like. Only by exploring unacknowledged exclusionary entry criteria and practices can we have a higher education system that is welcoming to all, rather than the few.

This can be done. An example from our own colleagues in the School of Education at Trinity College Dublin exemplifies this thinking and action. The Trinity Centre for People with Intellectual Disabilities (TCPID) is an internationally recognised and ground-breaking initiative that provides an education and work readiness programme for learners who have traditionally been excluded from higher education – even when other learners with a disability have been welcomed to our institutions. The programme and the Centre are neither a charity nor an advocacy. Rather, both are organised and assessed against the same quality assurance systems and academic rigour that all schools and departments in the College are held to. The Centre gives great expression to the philosophy and principles of UDL. With this focus, the learners are able to access the curriculum and demonstrate their knowledge and understanding in meaningful ways, and commence from College as educated and work-ready graduates, just like all of the other graduates from this prestigious institution. TCPID is a success because of leadership, vision, and the willingness to try (Aston, Shevlin, & Mc Guckin, 2019; Shevlin et al., 2020).

Until comparatively recently, learners from non-traditional groups attending HE were expected to assimilate and "fit in" to a system that was not designed with their needs or diversity in mind. Nor was there any real appreciation that all learners have different strengths, and consequently, variability was seen as the exception. Often it is thought that only those from marginalised groups, including individuals with disabilities, have different needs when it comes to their learning. This has resulted in a presumption that the changes that are occurring across higher education to make the system more inclusive will only benefit some learners, rather than a realisation that more inclusive practices benefit all learners and enable them to flourish and realise their potential.

Evolving Definitions of Inclusion

Like many areas in education, there is no universally agreed upon definition of inclusion, with a continuous debate in the literature regarding what it is, what it is not, and what it should be (e.g., Quirke & Mc Guckin, in press). What does appear to be agreed upon is that inclusion is underpinned by the notions of participation, human rights, social justice, and belonging.

Traditionally when we had to consider the concept of active inclusion and inclusive practice, the most obviously excluded group of learners were those who had a disability. Across recent times, we have come to realise that our widening participation initiatives really mean more than simply enabling other excluded groups of learners to access higher education. Getting access is only the beginning. Learners need to be enabled to progress through their studies and the wider experiences that we offer, and then to transfer to other courses or post qualifying lives of their choosing. As the diversity amongst the learner population increases and becomes more representative of society in general, there is a knock-on effect as each individual learner and cohort of learners expects and demands equality of access and equality of outcome. As a society we have become more vocal in voicing our wishes, desires, and concerns. The passivity that might have existed a generation or two ago has dissipated. With social and technological advances (e.g., social media), learners have a deeper appreciation of what exclusion and inclusion looks like, and with the global community becoming more like a village, there are greater levels of confidence for self and group advocacy.

As the old adage goes: travel broadens the mind. In higher education, we are exceptionally fortunate to be able to travel widely without having to leave work. The richness and diversity of our learner population is something to celebrate and learn from. With UDL as our travelling companion, we can both learn and act at the same time. Doing so will help us to recognise that inclusivity is a central component of everything we do, rather than being an "add-on" that perpetuates exclusionary practices.

Dr Cristina Devecchi reflects below on the Covid-19 pandemic and what it means for our definition of inclusion.

Dr Cristina Devecchi

Covid-19 has removed any doubt that failing to achieve rests only with a problem "within" the child or the adult. Years of austerity have impacted negatively on social services, the ability of local authorities to care and support, on health services, and on schools. While we are not out of the pandemic yet, the time is right to think again about inclusion and how to achieve it. So what next?

In 2005, while I was doing my PhD, I had the pleasure of working with Professor Lani Florian, who was editing the 1st Edition of *The Sage Handbook of Special Education* (Florian, 2005). The book opens with Florian's chapter titled "Reimagining Special Education". The title, the topic, and the hope for a different way of being inclusive caught my imagination.

Sadly, only five years later, a new government came into power in the UK. In setting out its programme for reform in education, it stated its intention to "remove the bias towards inclusion" (Cabinet Office, 2010, p. 29). Couched in the never abated debate about inclusion versus special education (see Florian, 2019; Warnock & Norwich, 2010), the consequences of that educational policy and others, such as the creation of "Academies", have put inclusion into reverse gear, to some extent. One such consequence has been the resurgence of a medical model, which serves the purpose of administering scarce resources (Florian et al., 2006) while blurring out of focus the socio-cultural and economic barriers many children face. Of course, social changes are never neat, and other models have continued to survive, but they do not shape policy. Paradoxically, the term "inclusion" has become a central concept and goal of UK policies in higher education, and of course a major driver in EU policies and the Sustainable Development Goals (SDGs).

Reflecting upon the concept of inclusion in education often results in the default position of "inclusive education", "special education", or other such initiatives within the classroom. This can result in inclusion being viewed narrowly and being mainly considered a school issue, and simply something that is related to accessing the curriculum. While access to the curriculum is essential, we need to expand our thinking and consider what inclusion should look like for us in higher education. An authentic approach to inclusion that is based on UDL can move the focus from individual learners to all learners, to all colleagues, and to all aspects of what we expect a higher education experience to encompass.

Inclusion in Practice

While we have set out the theoretical thinking about a UDL campus, the practice of inclusion necessitates consideration from a range of perspectives. This is where challenge can occur. It can be easy for the persuasiveness of a theoretical position to be agreed upon, but implementation and, moreover, continuous implementation, can be questioned. In the absence of an agreed upon operational definition, people resort to their own experience and personal understanding, resulting in implementation that can be ad-hoc and unpredictable. Whilst such natural instinct can be well intentioned, the subsequent results can lead to unintentional feelings and experiences of exclusion.

For successful practice, there needs to be institutional responsibility, professional responsibility, and most importantly, personal responsibility. Responsibility should be shared and should include the learner. While issues can arise that will necessitate professional intervention (e.g., from the Disability Officer or the IT department), the success of new UDL interventions will be determined by how they are actioned and accepted by others.

Take Some Time to Think

Andratesha Fritzgerald, Ed.S. Building Blocks of Brilliance, LLC, presents us with a very useful analogy of how change is constantly happening to us and, importantly, how we are not always aware that the change is happening. As reflexive practitioners, something that we scarcely do is to take the time to "stop and stand and stare" (Mc Guckin & O'Síoráin, 2021), suffering from the modern lifestyle "disease of being busy" (Safi, 2014).

Equity Well Check – Andratesha Fritzgerald

The eye alone
    May miss the entire
Picture –
        Without
                Correction.

I've worn glasses since I was in the third grade. I have always loved going to the eye doctor. Each time I go, I always expect for my prescription to remain intact. When I evaluate myself I feel like I can see fine. In my foggy estimation it seems like my vision is clear and unobstructed. When I don't feel any pain, I'm not squinting, and I'm not experiencing any discomfort – I make the false prognosis that I am seeing clearly and fully. When the doctor has me read the Eye Chart through the phoropter, the fancy name for the machine that eye doctors use to determine eyeglass prescriptions, I then start to gain perspective on what clarity truly is. My eyes alone cannot tell me whether I am seeing clearly, or if my vision needs correction – even if I have been through the full process every year since third grade. There is still correction needed.

The racism that is experienced by students of colour in higher education can go unnoticed and uncorrected if institutions don't commit to ongoing examination and the actions of correcting the vision to see it and eliminate it. Institutions of higher learning have to listen to the learners who are truly experts of their own experience to get a full diagnostic report of how clearly what they see aligns with what learners are experiencing. The *Journal of Blacks in Higher Education* found that the "retention rate", which is the percentage of first-time students who enter college and return to that same college for their second year, is 62.2% for all White students, but 52.1% for Black students (Racial Differences in College Persistence and Retention Rates, 2019). Did you blink twice to see if there was a need for corrective lenses? Just a little over half of Black students who entered at one college returned to that same college for year two. Has the university asked why? Or with the wink of an eye and the wipe of a lens has it been determined to keep moving forward with business as usual? There is a great need for examination. In the *Higher Education Today*, one study indicated that "[i]f new students do not experience a sense of belonging within eight weeks of arriving at college, they will be at high risk of dropping out" (Shaewitz & Crandall, 2020). The study goes on to share that 25% of first-time students with disabilities drop out by the end of year one and 35% drop out by year two. Imagine, for a moment, what colleges and universities are like for those who experience the intersectionality of being students who are both Black or disabled. Are universities ready for the examination that will show that there must be a change to the lenses we are evaluating institutions through if we truly want to become inclusive, antiracist, and welcoming?

In my book *Antiracism and Universal Design for Learning*, I share about the need for radical reform in both instructional design and systems. "Antiracism must be active, not passive. Universal design has to be intentionally implemented – not just intended. Success for all must be more than passion. It has to be power by empowerment!" (Fritzgerald, 2020). If higher education rests on the laurels of tradition and gatekeeping then the numbers for both students who are Black and who are disabled will continue to hide a dirty little secret – university is not designed for the success of either. And if a statement of such power causes shaking heads and dismissal, then the outcomes will remain the same if the practices do. What needs to change in higher education? Universal Design for Learning needs to be embedded in the design of courses. There needs to be explicit design that normalises support in the learning environment, not just at the learning centre, tutoring centre, or testing centre. The universal supports need to be explicitly embedded into the system instead of advancing racist and ableist rhetoric that teaches to a culture that does not match the entirety of the student body. There must be more co-creation of norms and expectations that invite every student into a position of power, thereby honouring their culture, their expectations, and their strengths. For far too long higher education has touted "high standards" as a code for "we keep in who we want to keep in and keep out who we want to keep out". The standards can remain high, but the pathway has to be customisable and fortified with supports that inherently change the face of who gets there, who stays, who is successful, and who ultimately graduates.

Every year since the third grade, I submit to an eye exam, because more outcomes for clear vision are met when I listen intently to one with experience and expertise. I implore universities to ask themselves the following questions to see if a new check-up strategy is needed:

1   Do our policies communicate a commitment to antiracism and anti-ableism? Is there a document with a public commitment to accountability in the area of antiracism? When is the last time there was a review of current policies through the lenses of antiracism and anti-ableism? What were the findings, and more importantly, what were the connected actions and commitments?

2   Has there been a data review with a particular emphasis on outcomes for students of colour and Indigenous and traditionally marginalised people groups? What were the findings and does the data hurt enough for us to make changes in policies, procedures, and practices that are producing the outcomes?

3   Have you asked students/alumni of colour and students with disabilities for feedback on their experiences at the university? Have you implemented changes based on their voices? Is there a commitment to invite their voices and other traditionally marginalised people groups to the decision-making process?

4   In 2020, the African American Student Union at the Harvard Graduate School of Design issued a list of action steps to address the institutionalised racism they faced as students. From their list, some ideas have been adapted to equip leaders to think through and truly examine where there are catalysts and connections for the work of antiracism and anti-oppression to start and or continue (Smithson, 2020).

Are voices of Black, gay, disabled, Indigenous people reflected in the curriculum? Are there diverse teachers and leaders in our system? Why or why not?

Has there been a concerted effort to have continuing self-reflective conversations about anti-racist policies and practices?

Are we acknowledging the work of promoting justice in meaningful ways within the system?

Do we include speakers who model academic excellence and attainment for diverse people groups?

Does the system value and protect those who speak out against racism, racist jokes, racist comments, and oppression of any kind?

Is there diversity in the representation of students receiving honours and academic accolades?

Does every student have knowledge of, and access to, the tools, resources, and supports for success? How do you know?

Is there a real connection to the community? Are diverse people welcome in your school or school system? Has there been a concerted effort to gain insight from all people to design curricula, systems, supports, or resources?

These questions are your Eye Chart.

Every organisation is called to decide which question they can answer clearly. If the vision is blurry and the answers are not apparent, then that is an indication that there is inequity that has been hidden in plain sight. I still wear glasses to this day. There is a need for me to submit to examination every year, and even sometimes more often. There are some issues with my eyes that have been prevented because I am a student of the regular check-up. It does not matter how much I think I know about my eyes or how well I see in my own humble opinion. That does not change the need for me to be examined, checked, evaluated, and corrected. And so it is the same with organisations. Antiracism is not a one-time statement, or an event that celebrates one Black person. It is the ongoing submission to check if our outcomes for all students match the intent of the actions we take. My eyes have taught me a lesson that there are some conditions that lenses cannot correct. Some issues in equity require dismantling, akin to surgery and others require a change in prescriptive action. Whatever the changes are, if higher education is an entity that is open to all, then it must be reflective of the practices that lead to success for all. In equity, we cannot always believe what we see. We must look and listen to those whose experiences and expertise will set us on a path of clarity with correction. Inequity that manifests as racism seems invisible until we tune our eyes to see it. Tuning our eyes to see inequity lasts as long as any organisation does. Will you believe the voices, the experience, and the expertise of those who have been marginalised and pushed out? What will be done to create change today? What will be done systematically and individually tomorrow? What will serve as evidence of a long-term commitment? What can each institute of higher learner commit to forever?

> The eye alone
>   May miss the entire
> Picture –
>   Without
>   Correction.
>   Check-up Needed.

Conclusion

The inclusion agenda has taken on added significance within higher education since the turn of the century. Having set out the philosophy and a practice of UDL in previous chapters, it is increasingly apparent that the embedding of such an approach also necessitates a continuous responsive from everyone, remembering that it is a journey rather than a destination.

This is because to be truly inclusive is very human and also means intentionally adapting and responding to the continually changing needs of an increasingly diverse learner "people". While UDL was originally associated with disability and issues relating to teaching practice, it is now regarded as a useful approach to frame inclusion practices, particularly at times when there is greater need for "innovation in inclusion theory" that will take into account all of the vagaries of the higher education system.

The world of learning changed dramatically with Covid-19. Until that time, inclusion was of interest but was on the edge, targeted at particular populations. Not everyone believed it to be their business and felt that some change was perhaps unnecessary or undoable and opted out. Recent experience of the pandemic and other global events have served, in a positive way, to shift thinking around educational inclusion. Everyone has had to redesign their engagement with not just their learners but their colleagues and their work. Moreover, there needs to be an ongoing "check in", as higher education continues to respond to both the changing world and new approaches to "inclusion".

Points to Consider

- Has your thinking about inclusion shifted in recent times? What has been the biggest learning for you and your work from the experience of the pandemic?
- Take a moment to reflect on your experiences of inclusion and exclusion – how might they frame your approach to inclusive practice for others?
- Do you now consider inclusion to be much broader than you might have previously considered?

References

Aston, D., Shevlin, M., & Mc Guckin, C. (2019). Trinity centre for people with intellectual disabilities. *Guidance Matters*, 2, 39–42. (ISSN: 2009-6941). Available at: http://hdl.handle.net/2262/91511

Cabinet Office. (2010). *The coalition: Our programme for government.* Retrieved from: https://webarchive.nationalarchives.gov.uk/ukgwa/20121015000000/http://www.direct.gov.uk/prod_consum_dg/groups/dg_digitalassets/@dg/@en/documents/digitalasset/dg_187876.pdf

Florian, L. (Ed.). (2005). *The SAGE handbook of special education.* London, UK: Sage.

Florian, L. (2019). On the necessary co-existence of special and inclusive education. *International Journal of Inclusive Education*, 23(7–8), 691–704. https://doi.org/10.1080/13603116.2019.1622801

Florian, L., Hollenweger, J., Simeonsson, R. J., Wedell, K., Riddell, S., Terzi, L., & Holland, A. (2006). Cross-cultural perspectives on the classification of children with disabilities: Part I. Issues in the classification of children with disabilities. *The Journal of Special Education, 40*(1), 36–45. https://doi.org/10.1177/00224669 060400010401

Fritzgerald, A. (2020). *Antiracism and universal design for learning: Building expressways to success.* Wakefield, MA: CAST, Incorporated.

Mc Guckin, C., & O'Síoráin, C. A. (2021). The professional self and diverse learning needs. In S. Soan (Ed.), *What do teachers need to know about diverse learning needs? Strengthening professional identity and well-being* (pp. 15–32). London: Bloomsbury Academic.

Quirke, M., & Mc Guckin, C. (in press). Watch your words! – Time to rethink our language for inclusion in education when using universal design approaches. *Frontiers in Education.*

Racial Differences in College Persistence and Retention Rates. (2019, July 22). *The Journal of Blacks in Higher Education.* Retrieved from: https://www.jbhe.com/ 2019/07/racial-differences-in-college-persistence-and-retention-rates/

Safi, O. (2014, November 6). The disease of being busy. [Blog post]. Retrieved from https://onbeing.org/blog/the-disease-of-being-busy/

Shaewitz, D., & Crandall, J. R. (2020, October 19). Higher education's challenge: Disability inclusion on campus. *Higher Education Today.* Retrieved from: https:// www.higheredtoday.org/2020/10/19/higher-educations-challenge-disability-inclusion-campus/

Shevlin, M., Kubiak, J., O'Donovan, M-A., Devitt, M., Ringwood, B., Aston, D., & Mc Guckin, C. (2020). Effective practices for helping students transition to work. In U. Sharma & S. Salend (Eds), *The encyclopedia of inclusive and special education.* Print: Oxford: Oxford University Press; Online: Oxford: Oxford Research Encyclopedia of Education. https://doi.org/10.1093/acrefore/9780190264093. 013.1234 Available at: http://www.tara.tcd.ie/handle/2262/93725

Smithson, A. (2020, June 17). Black students demand action on institutionalized whiteness at Harvard's graduate school of design. *The Architect's Newspaper.* Retrieved from: https://www.archpaper.com/2020/06/black-students-demand-action-on-institutionalized-racism-harvards-graduate-school-of-design/

Warnock, M., & Norwich, B. (2010). *Special educational needs: A new look.* London: Continuum.

Chapter 7

Redesigning Our Approaches
"Giving It a Go from the Get-Go"

Inclusion can no longer be only available for particular groups of learners in our institutions – it is now something that the entire academic community needs to be engaged in. To do this in a meaningful way, we must encourage and facilitate a new conversation with ourselves, our colleagues, and our learners. It would be wonderful to open up this conversation to those family, friends, and supporters who are not traditionally viewed as being members of our learning environments. And, why should they not have a voice in this important conversation? Should we exclude them? If so, for what valid reason?

Primary and post-primary schools have long understood that a well-developed policy, with everyone's voice being heard, leads to good practice and subsequent beneficial effects on experiences and outcomes. These schools have also recognised that prevention and intervention approaches need to be much wider than a "a whole school approach", acknowledging the wider ecology of their pupils, and necessitating "a whole community approach". Surely we should learn and act on this knowledge from the school sector? We are, after all, one community. If our higher education institutions are to authentically represent the society in which we live, then these more encompassing approaches need to be considered. What is to fear from a wide and inclusive conversation? The academic freedom that we so passionately defend is under no threat. Rather, true academic freedom recognises that, for dialogue and debate, higher education institutions should not be safe spaces.

And so, how do we do this? How do we "walk-the-walk" of active inclusion, and not just "talk-the-talk"? How do we include our learners and their supporters in this wider conversation, whilst also leading the way? In this chapter, we present four examples from colleagues who have explored UDL-led changes to their practice. Each of these contributions demonstrates that there is no right way to think about how UDL can be used in your work. Evident in each example is that the UDL journey required some personal reflection and thinking about the person's own outlook on life and mindset, with authentic conversations and sharing of the learning process. If we reduce the conversation about UDL to being only about teaching, learning, and assessment, then we

DOI: 10.4324/9781003137672-8

will miss the real potential of what UDL can provide. We will miss out on the opportunity to embed UDL thinking and practice across all aspects of our higher education institutions. After all, inclusion is also about the wider learner experience. A reductionist approach to only teaching, learning, and assessment activities will likely lead to an approach where activities are changed for the sake of saying that they were changed, with a template and checklist approach. Very quickly, we would see a reporting tool or dashboard where inclusion and UDL would become just another facile metric on our campuses – things getting done simply because they are being counted. What could be more anti-inclusion than this type of approach? We hope that these examples will support you in developing your confidence to explore how UDL can be a benefit to you – at both a personal and a professional level. Embarking on any new journey can be both exciting and nervous at the same time. Have a look at the examples and see if they can give you the courage and motivation to "have-a-go from the get-go".

Applying UDL: Three Examples

The first example, from Emma Whewell, reflects on how Emma and her colleagues in a Sport and Exercise department explored UDL as a means to break down barriers for under-represented and marginalised groups in education. Through a process of being open to what learners had to say, the working group developed a culture of "no assumptions". With this openness, there was real potential to build on, and embed, the UDL concept of "Self-Regulation". Whilst Emma reflects on what they did at a departmental level, Carrie Archer shares her experience of how colleagues from across various departments and service areas can come together as a community to support each other in their professional development. Carrie demonstrates that UDL can be a shared mindset across disciplines and different parts of the institution, with some people doing it because they need to, and others doing it because they want to. Considering that very few of us ever really work completely independently of colleagues in our own area, or across the institution, we can naturally feel fearful of feeling vulnerable and sharing such work in an environment that is often fraught with personal and group dynamics. Carrie's example shows how we can encourage and support UDL (e.g., multiple means of engagement) across a Community of Practice (CoP) by moving away from the "silo approach" that many of us experience in our institutions. In the third example, Catherine O'Reilly, a former pre-school teacher, shares her personal reflection on how she encountered UDL after she commenced her doctoral research journey. As a reflexive researcher and practitioner, Catherine reflects upon how she internalised UDL at both a personal and professional level, enacting thinking and changes in her research and practice. Catherine is an example of "having a go from the get-go". In the fourth example, Dr. Carol-Ann O'Sioráin invites you to engage in a reflective excercise. This is an opportunity to be reflexive in your own professional practice – having considered the other examples – an opportunity to be mindful as you engage in a personal learning and 'design for inclusion'.

Breaking Down Barriers

Emma Whewell

This example has been provided by Emma Whewell, a Physical Education specialist. Emma is Associate Professor in Teaching and Learning at the University of Northampton, and is the Deputy Subject Leader for Sport and Exercise. In their work to break down barriers for under-represented and marginalised groups in education, Emma and colleagues developed a culture of "no assumptions" to build on the UDL concept of "Self-Regulation".

As part of the University of Northampton's *Access and Participation Plan (APP)*, the Sport and Exercise department has been working on breaking down barriers for under-represented and marginalised groups in education. In the APP report, these include white working-class males; black; Asian and minority ethnic; mature; disabled; care leavers; service families; and intersections of disadvantage. The APP had a focus upon attainment, non-continuation, and access and progression to further employment or study.

This vignette focuses upon some of the work undertaken by the *Breaking Down Barriers* working group to consider what would make the experiences of Sport and Exercise learners more inclusive and relevant. In "thinking about" inclusion and inclusive practices, we decided to work with our learner representatives to gain an understanding of the barriers experienced in accessing learning, teaching, and assessment in Sport and Exercise. Our starting point was one of developing a culture of "no assumptions". This means that we do not assume prior knowledge, prior experience, prior understanding, or prior achievement.

Learners reported feelings of being unable to access the content of some teaching sessions, where assumptions had been made in relation to their knowledge and experiences. In particular, this was related to the clarity of vocabulary, syntax, and structure used.

Assumptions had been made that all learners would understand, interpret, and access the information presented in the same way. The use and choice of language and examples used alienated the learners who did not understand the meaning, context, and vocabulary presented. In our culture of "no assumptions", we pre-teach key vocabulary and present definitions and context for technical and key words. These are presented in written, verbal, and symbolic form. Colleagues are expected to check for misconceptions and present complex information in a relevant context.

Similarly, the entry route of our learners is varied, in terms of quality, qualifications, and experiences. Learners reported that they felt they needed support in understanding and applying complex concepts in a way that is relevant to them. This was particularly apparent in the resources associated with contemporary and critical issues in Sport and Exercise: race, gender, sexuality, ethnicity, and socio-economic background. Learners' prior experiences influenced the ways in which they were able to access and understand the context of the resources provided. In our culture of "no assumptions", colleagues are expected to contextualise information through "big idea" concepts. There are "Multiple Representations" of concepts that are culturally and learner relevant. We present a decolonised curriculum which invites learners to explore across cultures and experiences. Presentations draw upon key ideas that are substantial in developing understanding and context.

We have found that careful consideration of the relevance of the materials used in sessions is important to the engagement and interactions of our learners. Using meaningful and valuable resources and content provides a personalised context that is socially relevant to our learners. We draw upon a wide range of research, and athletic and athlete case studies that represent a versatile body of resources. In turn, we offer our learners autonomy in their assessments, facilitating them to choose how best to contextualise their discussion. This is a fundamental component of UDL. We encourage learners to draw from a representative body of research and to apply this to their own relevant examples. This has improved opportunities for peer interaction, debate, and discussion that builds understanding and community.

Assessment and feedback was highlighted by our learners as an area of dissatisfaction. They reported that feedback was not always helpful or specific enough, and that examples of correct practice or resources would be useful. Our culture of "no assumptions" permeates our feedback and assessments. Drawing upon UDL, we now offer multiple mechanisms across the degree programmes for learners to demonstrate their attainment. Our assessment portfolio is wide and includes a range of methods including posters, presentations, clinical examples, videos, practical assessments, debates, and essays. Colleagues are expected, in their feedback, not to assume understanding – feedback is constructed in a manner that is purposeful and contains feed-forward mechanisms and signposting to support the learner. Words such as "good" have been contextualised and qualified in the feedback comments. We are in the process of trialling video and audio feedback. Our aim is to offer "Mastery" orientated feedback, which does not focus on relative performance, and more on positive strategies for future success.

The range of experiences reported by our learners brings with it a range of motivations to study. We have focussed our efforts in taught sessions and within the personal tutoring system to build on the UDL concept of "Self-Regulation". Self-regulation is important in fostering a learning environment where learners feel safe and able to cope. Our personal tutoring system supports learners to set goals and targets that are personal and relevant to them. Goals are a combination of what it is we want to do and what it is we need to do. Our culture of "no assumptions" means that our staff work with our students to develop skills of self-organisation, planning for study, and a space for shared reflection. In taught sessions, we encourage the challenges that group work, presenting, and debating can present and plan explicitly teaching these skills.

The *Breaking Down Barriers* group has been in place for a year now and has plans to further develop the successful strategies seen to date. Ideas that we have been "thinking about" include developing the use of assistive technologies, particularly in our laboratory-based and clinical sessions. We also aim to address the current issue of progression on the degree programmes – this is particularly low in the group of learners that the APP report identified as being at risk. We are discussing ways in which we can demonstrate connections between degree content – across modules and in real-life situations (e.g., work placements) to allow learners to apply their learning to a range of contexts. In some of our work, the influence and use of UDL is very obvious. In other places, it is much more subtle. With a focus on "no assumptions", we all had to be open to a certain level of feeling exposed. UDL thinking made this okay – encouraging us all to support an open approach to exploring how we can best help our learners. I think that, at both a personal and professional level, each of us has learnt a bit more about being inclusive.

In this example from Emma, curriculum and assessment issues were considered to ensure accessibility to learning. Moreover, concepts such as "motivation to learn", "self-regulation", and "thinking about technologies" were important in ensuring that all learners felt comfortable, considered, and had a sense of belonging in their learning. The objective to engage a diversity of learners involved a deeper consideration of what contributes to inclusion. There was a clear recognition that inclusion is more than a reflection of the curriculum and assessment, greater than a checklist and embedded in the culture of a department.

The challenge for all of us is to embed this approach and thinking within and across all parts of our higher education institutions. Whilst Emma and colleagues were all from the same discipline area, implementing a UDL approach might require the input of colleagues from a wide range of areas in the institution. The next example sets out how establishing a Community of Practice (CoP) can create some protected time to rethink and redesign our learning spaces. It sets out how each of us can lead this dialogue from within, if our hope is for a learning environment where all of our learners and colleagues are to thrive in a truly inclusive UDL environment that continuously evolves.

Carrie Archer is the Professional Learning and Development Officer for the City of Dublin Education and Training Board (CDETB) in Ireland. Carrie is also involved in teacher education for Further Education and Training (FET) educators in a number of higher education institutions in Dublin, most specifically in the areas of diversity and inclusion. Through her varied roles, Carrie aims to encourage, facilitate, promote, and model a strong culture of professional dialogue, learning, and development through each and every action and interaction.

Learning Together in a Community of Practice

Carrie Archer

The notion of a Community of Practice (CoP) challenges the long-held view that learning is something that is an individualistic endeavour. Lave and Wenger (1991) remind us that learning is a social process that is situated in a cultural and historical context. For our work in higher education and UDL, a CoP can be of great help. They have the potential to bring together colleagues and friends from our own and disparate areas of work, all to either create something entirely new or solve a common problem (Farnsworth, Kleanthous, & Wenger-Trayner, 2016).

CoPs are shared social spaces (physical or virtual) where collective and negotiated learning takes place, where there is a focus on a similar goal or passion, a domain, or a joint enterprise. In terms of contributions, members of a CoP are accountable to themselves and to each other. Participation in a CoP involves regular interaction and engagement to share learning, with members becoming competent in the use of a shared range of resources (Wenger, McDermott, & Snyder, 2002).

Effective CoPs are participant-led, with the goals and agenda developing organically in a shared, safe, yet challenging space. Through reflective dialogue, members critically analyse and evaluate current practices, all with the intent of shaping attitudes and beliefs as well as knowledge (McElearney, Murphy, & Radcliffe, 2019). When consciously gathering as a collective in a CoP, it "...shapes the way we think, feel and make sense of our world" (Parker, 2018, p. 3). Gathering provides opportunities to talk about ideas; to share information; to test ways of being in the world, in teaching spaces, in staff-rooms and institutions; and even to explore what it is that the world needs. Who is included, who is invited, and who is at the table at gatherings can influence and impact on the direction that these discussions take. Reflective dialogue allows members to listen, to share insights and collective knowledge, and to openly and actively question and challenge beliefs in an unbiased way, all with the overall intention of improving experiences for learners (Dogan, Yurtseven, & Tatık, 2019). Social contracts are drawn when people gather. Sometimes these are explicit, and sometimes they are implicit. Not only do they address the question of what individuals get from the gathering, but they also examine what each is expected to contribute, to offer, and to give (Parker, 2018).

CoPs are of immediate interest to anyone on an inclusion journey (e.g., see Quirke, Mc Guckin, & McCarthy, 2022). Central to this journey is the understanding that, individually, we each need to check-in on our attitudes and beliefs about our own abilities to support learners with barriers to learning or additional needs, and about the learners' cognitive abilities and potential to learn (Hart, Dixon, Drummond, & McIntyre, 2004). Sharing insights and collective knowledge on what impacts on the learning process allows for discussion on what works and what does not work, and how members of the CoP might address these (Horn & Little, 2010). Inclusive pedagogical approaches reject "labelling" of learners and support the assertion that any approaches that were traditionally made available to support a few learners should be open and available to all (Florian & Spratt, 2013). This is central to a UDL mindset and removes any limits that might be placed on learners. An assumed limit on learner ability can quickly become a self-fulfilling prophecy about what we deem to be "appropriate" learning experiences (Hart et al., 2004). The same is true of how we view and perceive ourselves as educators. Cognition, emotion, and motivation are three dimensions which determine educator behaviour, and affective and motivational drivers are important (Damasio, 1994; Järvilehto, 2001).

Collective efficacy (CE) is the shared belief among a group of educators that they have what it takes to accomplish the complex and challenging mission of genuinely and impactfully reaching, teaching, and positively influencing every learner (Tschannen-Moran & Barr, 2004). When working with challenging learners, a sense of CE among the individuals in the group leads to the belief that they can do it, that "they've got this". If an individual has the belief that they can do something, they are likely to be more engaged and more motivated to do it, impacting positively on perseverance and effort (DeWitt, Donohoo, & Tschannen-Moran, 2021). These are all key elements when we consider the UDL guidelines underpinning "Multiple Means of Engagement". If this is true for educators, it is also true for learners. When a collective shares a belief, it has the potential to impact on individual learners, classrooms, faculties, and entire institutions (Darling-Hammond, Hyler, & Gardner, 2017).

CoPs have a shared empathy. If a member encounters some difficulty or failure with trialling a new approach, then the shared resilience can reframe the experience and present it as an opportunity for reflection and growth (Donohoo, Hattie, & Eells, 2018). This is a hugely important point. When we accept and acknowledge that none of us is perfect, then we reduce the pressure that we often feel at work to get everything right on the first try, and that the inability to do so is failure. When trying UDL and sharing with colleagues, we need to feel that we have a safe and respectful "space" to try, to fail, to try again, and to have a go! CE becomes strengthened with the celebration of mastery experiences within the group. When celebrating and sharing mastery experiences, other members of the group see this success, and the success spreads! It can be positively infectious!

Vicarious learning takes place within a CoP. There is a sense of excitement and through these experiences, other individuals in the group believe that they can do this too (Bandura, 1977). When the collective verbally persuade each other that reaching all learners is possible, that together, the group have "got this", and what is articulated is what will manifest (DeWitt et al., 2021), such networks provide colleagues with the relationships and interpersonal interactions that they need, where practice is shared, discussed, and critiqued in a collaborative and reflective manner (de Neve, Devos, & Tuytens, 2015).

As with all group activities, there is always the potential hazard of groupthink. Groupthink occurs when the members of a group all begin to think alike, do not challenge each other, and where reflective dialogue is limited or absent. It can arise for several reasons. For example, if there is a "fixed mindset" (as opposed to a growth mindset) within the group, groupthink can evolve (Dweck, 2012). Boundaries within a group can also create groupthink or create too narrow a focus or limit expectations. Barriers might be set up because of who is included in the group membership. It is widely acknowledged that power relations are inherent in education and can shape our interactions with each other (Farnsworth et al., 2016). Additionally, if a leader begins to emerge within the collective who dominates, they can punish what is viewed as dissent if members challenge their thinking. They may try to silence perceived dissenters, or even remove them from the group (Dweck, 2012). New members to an established CoP may be on probation, and if they feel that their competence is not enough, or if a culture does not exist which is supportive of them, they can feel marginalised and not contribute (Farnsworth et al., 2016). Furthermore, if a member is seen as being a genius, others may follow their lead and question their own value, input, and ability, falling in line behind the genius (Dweck, 2012). This could clip the wings of other members, resulting in marginalisation (Farnsworth et al., 2016; Wenger, 2016). Whilst these are all things to be mindful of, they are certainly not unsurmountable.

Evaluating the impact of professional learning on learner outcomes and the knowledge–practice gap for educators is both complex and challenging. Educators need support to truly embed professional learning into practice, and CoPs or collaborative practices and learning cultures can help sustain changes to practice following professional development activities over time (King, 2014, 2016). The most effective CoPs are ones where senior leadership in the institution support the CoP proactively and intentionally, and where CE can thrive (Donohoo, O'Leary, & Hattie, 2020). This includes creating time and space for gathering within the normal routine of the week or semester, where the CoP is valued as an integral element of professional learning and development. In conclusion, if we want to believe that we have the competence and potential to reach all of our learners, to overcome barriers, to meet with challenges, and to truly improve outcomes for our learners, then building safe, shared spaces to engage in collective, reflective dialogue is key.

The examples from Emma and Carrie are probably more meaningful to any of us with a formal role in our institutions that relates to the learner experience. However, many of our colleagues have no learner-facing role, being engaged in research and other support activities. In the following example, Catherine reflects upon her introduction to the UDL concept, and how this has led to some reflexive thinking and changes to her research approach and applied practice. With a wealth of experience as a practitioner in early childhood educational studies, Catherine reflects that whilst she knew about inclusion in education and teaching, the introduction of UDL presented challenges to this previous knowledge and posed new queries as to whether UDL had a role in her new life as a researcher. From first-hand experience, Catherine has been able to see that UDL really does need a change in attitude and mindset.

The Emerging Researcher

Catherine O'Reilly

My research story has a beginning, a middle, and an end, and like all good stories, the ending is not an end, rather it is a new beginning. So let us begin!

This story is set within the landscape of Early Childhood Education and Care. I started my research journey in 2014 when I enrolled as a mature student on a BA (Hons) in Early Childhood Education and Care course. Upon completing this course in 2017, I had yet to be introduced to the mysterious concept of UDL. In 2018, I enrolled for a Master's Degree in Leadership in Early Childhood Education and Care. This innovative and exciting course included the first "Children's Rights" module in Ireland that specifically focused on children during early childhood (i.e., aged 0–6). Other modules in this course included entrepreneurship and contemporary issues in early childhood curriculum theory and practice, yet on completion of this course in 2019, the enigmatic concept of UDL remained absent from classroom discussions. So, are we to assume that UDL is not part of early childhood educational studies?

But then, one day in September 2020, I enrolled for a PhD and along comes UDL. As I have indicated, UDL was a new concept for me, even though I could identify with many of its principles. For example, awareness of pedagogy that supports inclusion and additional needs are part of the daily life of a preschool educator. However, is it a part of being a researcher? I wasn't sure.

To find out more, I engaged in online seminars provided by the School of Education's Inclusion in Education and Society (IES) Research Group. Facilitated by Patricia McCarthy and Mary Quirke, these seminars provided me with the opportunity to hear about the challenges others face in their research activities and in their participation in society. Additionally, I enrolled in a Trinity module to gain further insights into "The Why", "The What", and "The How" of UDL, and how it might fit into my own professional development. The module was called Trinity-INC (Inclusive Curriculum) Professional Learning Module in Inclusive Practices for Teaching and Learning, and its purpose was to expose learners to issues of inclusion and diversity, where participants are invited to engage in critical discourse.

After engaging in the research discussions during the IES seminars and the Trinity-INC sessions, I began to understand that UDL is much more than a broad concept; rather, for me, it seemed to be more about adopting and implementing principles of best practice. I was further exposed to the practice of UDL as a volunteer and committee member of the Annual Postgraduate Research Conference in the School of Education at Trinity College Dublin. Here I experienced first-hand the complexity of adopting a UDL mindset. My first intentional active practice of UDL was during the conference when I volunteered to support research students in designing and submitting research posters, to be exhibited online, using a UDL approach. This concept proved much more challenging than I anticipated. Even when provided with clear guidelines on how to submit an accessible online poster, research students struggled to make their posters accessible to viewers with mixed abilities. Some students tried many times, and others found it easier to use the format they were familiar with and hoped for the best. Thus, I began to understand UDL not only as a model for best practice but also as an attitude and mindset. This experience impacted my thinking and approach as a researcher and, moreover, a professional with responsibilities to the early childhood sector. Therefore, I decided to re-think my PhD research design and to be proactive in adopting a UDL mindset.

My research involves design-based research where I will develop an intervention drawing from the concept of oral storytelling to draw out pre-schoolers' emerging critical thinking skills. However, I had not considered UDL as part of my research design. To be honest, at the time, my thoughts were, "Well, that's someone else's field; I have enough theories to be thinking about". This is no longer the case! Thus, reflecting on my learning and professional growth over the past year, I now intend to incorporate UDL by providing participants with "Multiple Means of Engagement and Representation". I will do this by consulting with them on the research design and engaging in reflexive critical discourse to unpack what we are doing as a group, and to find the best solutions – drawing from the participants' contributions and interweaving this with my responsibility to address the research aims and objectives of the study.

This is my new beginning, the start of a new story that I accredit to the impact of engaging with UDL as a way to ensure my research is steeped in best practice. By reflecting on the principles of UD and UDL and taking this reflection into my conversations with my supervisors, my research study group, and my life, I believe I have already improved the quality of my thinking, learning, and teaching going forward. If you wish to know what changes I made to my research, my thesis will tell that story!

Catherine's example is a useful reminder that UDL can be a personal journey even for educators with formal education and training in inclusive pedagogic practices. The UDL approach to the research process increases, easily and effectively, the ability for research participants to more fully engage in, and participate in, meaningful research and data collection.

Seeing Yourself as a UDL Apprentice

From the previous examples we can see that we are all apprentices and "having a go from the get-go" is important. We cannot be master craftsmen without serving an apprenticeship and working steadily on increasing your competence and confidence with our craft. Does anyone ever become the master? Every day is a school day. *Is* there a guru? If there is, is this hierarchical and more about power than collegiality? If someone professes to know everything about UDL and active inclusion, is this the emperor's new clothes? Regardless of how expert we are seen in our own areas, the nature of higher education is that we are always advancing new knowledge – and if we are to put some "inclusion" into learning we also need to reflect on our own teaching practice in higher education (O'Síoráin et al., 2021), as highlighted in our next case example from Dr Carol-Ann O'Síoráin.

Carol-Ann is Assistant Professor of Early Childhood Education in the Institute of Education at Dublin City University (DCU) in Ireland. Through her academic and applied work, Carol-Ann encourages educators to reflect upon and be reflexive regarding their professional development and pedagogical approaches. In doing so, Carol-Ann argues that this reflexive practice facilitates inclusive learning and learner engagement.

Reaching with Your Teaching

Dr Carol-Ann O'Síoráin

In this section, I invite you to engage in a reflection exercise as a teacher, on "teaching" in higher education using UDL. The aim of this exercise is to enable you, both as a reader and as a teacher, to step back and review how you develop and build inclusive approaches into your daily teaching practice.

The first task is to invite you to disentangle yourself from any perceptions you have created about what you think a UDL approach in teaching is about. Across all institutions at higher level, and other partners in teacher education, there is a growing emphasis on widening opportunities for greater access in a variety of modes, whether physical infrastructure, curriculum, education practice, policy, or legislation. Universal Design (UD) is frequently mentioned as a means by which to achieve this. As a teacher educator or practitioner there is constant focus now on applying UD principles to every aspect of our work, from content development, lectures, mentoring workshops, to assessments. This can feel over-whelming and I frequently hear colleagues mention that their approach is "UD'd" (presumably meaning that all bases are covered). This also presents challenges to professional confidence and competencies.

I recently took time to reflect on a personal but important role, my rugby tag coaching for children with additional needs. The team is a large group of players aged from 6 to 20 years, each with a diagnosed additional need. Some really want to play "rugby" and some just know that they are coming every Sunday to have fun. What matters is they are a team and Pat's idea of what "rugby" is can be very different to what Charlie's idea of what "rugby" is, but they both play "rugby". As a coach, when it comes to selecting the skills and training needed, we look at the player profile and make one small change. The task here is not to treat all of the players in the same way or with the same expectation. Each player has a great expectation of playing *their* "rugby". The one thing that we all do in unison is the warm-up exercises for our muscles and our bodies. This is where it is easy to see their motivation and the interpersonal relationships that promote scaffolding, encouragement, and success in their game. How do you UD that? Not all of us know where to start when learning to play a sport like rugby, or how to achieve personal success. So, let's focus on learning how to bake cookies!

Consider this next section as if you are learning something for the first time.

Pause for reflection: What image do you have of what your cookies will look like once baked?

Do you visualise them as all the same size, colour, or texture? Can you imagine the smell of them as they bake or cool? Are you already sorting in your head the decoration ideas or collating the list of possible ingredients?

Who might eat these cookies? What food intolerances or allergies will need to be considered? Who might wish to have tea or coffee with them?

Progression in inclusion and inclusive practice is everywhere in policy and accountability, and also in our personal and professional standards as educators and practitioners – even as rugby coaches. We must acknowledge our own evolving personal and professional identities, our "prevailing ideologies", and "de-centre from the accumulation of attitudes, perspectives, prejudices," and our reliable/habitual practices (O'Síoráin et al., 2021, p. 16). Mc Guckin and O'Síoráin (2021) argue that "...to be truly reflective, we need to be aware of the possible need to change our mindsets and approaches to practice" (p. 16).

So, as a teacher, as a teacher educator, and as a rugby coach, I invite you to take a step back for a moment and ask yourself a series of questions:

- What do I know about UDL?
- How might I build my inclusive practice in a way that reflects an organic approach?
- How will I enhance my practice over time?
- How will I develop quality learning experiences for my learners?
- How might I achieve "higher" inclusive outcomes?

As we start to consider our engagement with UDL, we need to start by asking ourselves, "what is universal about learning successfully?". Take a moment to consider this, maybe create a mind map or a spider diagram before you advance to my example below.

- Successful learning = learner/self-focused
  - Context:
    - Place in space
    - Physical self
    - Social self
    - Emotional self
    - Cultural self
    - Intellectual self
    - Environment
    - Past, present, and future
  - Comfortable self
    - Demanded of self
    - Challenged self
    - Aware of learning self
  - Practice makes perfect
    - Testing self
    - Say-it self
    - Do-it self
    - Practice, reflect, and adjust self

When we think about our learners, whether they are pre-schoolers, school-age children, teenagers, adult learners, or rugby players, whether they have additional learning needs or not, we must remind ourselves that they are constantly learning. They are learning both inside and outside of our classrooms, lecture halls, and pitches. Their lived experience and each of the relationships they engage with daily, their families, friends, colleagues – people in their lives and the wider world they engage with – is their bio-ecology. This ecology, as identified by Urie Bronfenbrenner, is also constantly changing and dynamic in nature.

So, as we continue to reflect on baking those cookies, take a further moment to reflect:

What prompted your interest in making the cookies?

Why learn this task at all (purposeful motivation)?

What motivated you to continue to learn this new skill until you could master it independently (motivation to be independent)?

Did you need to borrow or access any baking utensils or ingredients?

Did you need the assistance of another person to guide you, provide encouragement, physically assist you, or provide positive feedback (resourceful and knowledgeable)?

Did you understand the language and symbols within the recipe? Did it matter?

Can you remember:

- The strategies and goals that either you set for yourself or were set for you in the recipe?
- The effort required to learn this new task?
- The positive and negative events that you may have experienced? If so, how did you persist if things went wrong?
- The attention needed when measuring ingredients and mixing dough, seeking the right consistency?
- Your physical body when applying the "rub-in" method, perhaps challenged if the work surface was too high, the bowl not steady and needing you to hold it against your body, or perhaps you were physically uncomfortable (needing the toilet, tired, under pressure or too hungry to wait!)?
- How your working memory assisted you the next time you made the cookies – appreciating the feel of the butter and flour as you

rubbed them together, knowing the amount of pressure necessary to bring the dough together? Remembering the adaptations
you made to your environment that made it easier the last time,
the setting of the oven temperature, the consistency of the
mixture?

Consider what you have you gained in expertise, how you shared
your culinary exploits with others and shared your recipe? Did you
upload it to social media?

Or perhaps you decided to make a change – a different mix and
flavour perhaps.

Who assisted you? Did you follow someone on YouTube or the
internet? Did their approach matter? Did it matter if their method
was different to yours? If they explained in a different language, used
ingredients not available to you, perhaps even called those cookies
"biscuits", did it matter? Should it?!

As teachers, practitioners, and rugby coaches what you need to
know as you approach UDL and inclusion, be it in your classroom,
lecture hall, or rugby pitch, is that there is a great diversity of lived
and learning experience already in the space. And you as a teacher,
educator, or coach need to acknowledge and appreciate that.

That is your starting point.

My reflections as I apply the UDL framework to my rugby coaching,
as I aim for successful inclusive learning/engagement/play, have three
core elements for success:

1   Place and space: this builds student/player identity and agency in
    valuing self to be purposeful and motivated in learning, play, and
    life. They are engaged in the "why of learning" or the "why of the
    sport".
2   Past, present, and future: students/players are confident, compe-
    tent, resourceful, and knowledgeable to be independent at "having
    a go" and bringing a task to an agreed result (a pulled tag, pass
    the ball to a teammate, or a try!). They understand and present
    the "what of learning" or the "what of playing".
3   Practice makes perfect: students/players can make advances,
    adapt to challenges, build fluency in practice and presentation,
    monitor their own achievements, and set new goals. They volun-
    teer the "how of learning" or the "how of the game".

So, what kind of rugby will they play? They'll play "their rugby", or and they'll eat your cookies if they like the look, the shape, the taste, and the smell of them. They'll also tell you how you might improve your recipe ... if you ask them!

Conclusion

In this chapter, we have drawn on the work of colleagues to demonstrate how it is timely for all of us involved in higher education to recognise that we all need to be part of the wider discussion about inclusion, and how UDL can be a useful approach to guide these new conversations and developments, regardless of the role that each of us has in higher education. As for our learners, there is no one group of colleagues that need to be more included than the other. Such an approach leads to exclusion, and the circle of exclusion will only continue. The examples in this chapter demonstrate how UDL is for everyone, and that a UDL journey is not simply about using a template or checklist to check or change what we do. Rather, the most beneficial approach is to see this UDL journey as both a chance to review our own personal view of the world and the work that we are doing. Such a reflexive approach can help us all to examine if we are truly being inclusive in both thinking and action. It would, after all, be a bit strange to lay claim to being inclusive in our work, but not inclusive in our thinking and work beyond the institution!

Points to Consider

- Sometimes it can feel that other people make the task look easy – but can you identify your own skills and competencies that would enable you to develop your confidence for your UDL work?
- Take a moment to reflect on what your personal motivators are for your work. How could these translate into drivers for further developing your UDL and inclusion work?
- Working with others can be fun! Which colleague(s) would you like to join you in a Community of Practice?
- How could everyone in your institution share a consistent approach to develop and evolve the message of inclusion?

References

Bandura, A. (1977). Self-efficacy: Toward a unifying theory of behavioral change. *Psychological Review*, 84(2), 191–215. https://doi.org/10.1037/0033-295X.84.2.191

Damasio, A. R. (1994). *Descartes' error: Emotion, reason and the human brain.* New York, NY: Grosset Putman.

Darling-Hammond, L., Hyler, M. E., & Gardner, M. (2017). *Effective teacher professional development*. Palo Alto, CA: Learning Policy Institute.

de Neve, D., Devos, G., & Tuytens, M. (2015). The importance of job resources and self-efficacy for beginning teachers' professional learning in differentiated instruction. *Teaching and Teacher Education*, *47*, 30–41. https://doi.org/10.1016/j.tate.2014.12.003

DeWitt, P., Donohoo, J., & Tschannen-Moran, M. (2021). *Demystifying collective efficacy*. Corwin Leaders Coaching Leaders Podcast. https://youtu.be/ONlYiMOx-Ro

Dogan, S., Yurtseven, N., & Tatık, R. Ş. (2019). Meeting agenda matters: promoting reflective dialogue in teacher communities. *Professional Development in Education*, *45*(2), 231–249. https://doi.org/10.1080/19415257.2018.1474484

Donohoo, J., Hattie, J., & Eells, R. (2018). The power of collective efficacy. *Educational Leadership*, *75*(6), 40–44.

Donohoo, J., O'Leary, T., & Hattie, J. (2020). The design and validation of the enabling conditions for collective teacher efficacy scale (EC-CTES). *Journal of Professional Capital and Community*, *5*(2), 147–166. https://doi.org/10.1108/JPCC-08-2019-0020

Dweck, C. (2012). *Mindset: How you can fulfil your potential*. Hachette, London: Constable & Robinson Limited.

Farnsworth, V., Kleanthous, I., & Wenger-Trayner, E. (2016). Communities of practice as a social theory of learning: A conversation with Etienne Wenger. *British Journal of Educational Studies*, *64*(2), 139–160. https://doi.org/10.1080/00071005.2015.1133799

Florian, L., & Spratt, J. (2013). Enacting inclusion: a framework for interrogating inclusive practice. *European Journal of Special Needs Education*, *28*(2), 119–135. https://doi.org./10.1080/08856257.2013.778111

Hart, S., Dixon, A., Drummond, M. J., & McIntyre, D. (2004). *Learning without limits*. Buckingham, UK: Open University Press.

Horn, I. S., & Little, J. W. (2010). Attending to problems of practice: Routines and resources for professional learning in teachers' workplace interactions. *American Educational Research Journal*, *47*(1), 181–217. https://doi.org/10.3102/0002831209345158

Järvilehto, T. (2001). Feeling as knowing (Part 2): Emotion, consciousness, and brain activity. Consciousness & Emotion, 2, 75–102. https://doi.org/10.1075/ce.2.1.04jar

King, F. (2014). Evaluating the impact of teacher professional development: an evidence-based framework. *Professional Development in Education*, *40*(1), 89–111. https://doi.org/10.1080/19415257.2013.823099

King, F. (2016). Teacher professional development to support teacher professional learning: Systemic factors from Irish case studies. *Teacher Development*, *20*(4), 574–594. https://doi.org/10.1080/13664530.2016.1161661

Lave, J., & Wenger, E. (1991). *Situated learning: Legitimate peripheral participation*. Cambridge: Cambridge University Press. https://doi.org/10.1017/CBO9780511815355

McElearney, A., Murphy, C., & Radcliffe, D. (2019). Identifying teacher needs and preferences in accessing professional learning and support. *Professional Development in Education*, *45*(3), 433–455. https://doi.org/10.1080/19415257.2018.1557241

Mc Guckin, C., & O'Síoráin, C. A. (2021). The professional self and special and able and talented education. In S. Soan (Ed.), *Why do teachers need to know about diverse learning needs?* London: Bloomsbury.

O'Síoráin, C. A., Mc Guckin, C., & Carr-Fanning, K. (2021). Well that's another fine mess you got me into. In Alison Fox, Hugh Busher, & Carmel Capewell (Eds.), *Thinking critically and ethically about research for education: Engaging with voice and empowerment in international contexts* (pp. 40–53). London: Routledge.

Parker, P. (2018). *The art of gathering: how we meet and why it matters.* New York: Riverhead Books.

Quirke, M., Mc Guckin, C., & McCarthy, P. (2022). How to adopt an "inclusion as process" approach and navigate ethical challenges in research. In *SAGE Research Methods Cases.* London, United Kingdom: SAGE Publications, Ltd. https://doi.org/10.4135/9781529605341

Tschannen-Moran, M., & Barr, M. (2004). Fostering student learning: The relationship of collective teacher efficacy and student achievement. *Leadership and Policy in Schools, 3*(3), 189–209. https://doi.org/10.1080/15700760490503706

Wenger, E. (2016). Communities of practice and social learning systems. *Organization 7*(2), 225–246. https://doi.org/10.1177/135050840072002

Wenger, E., McDermott, R., & Snyder, W. (2002). *Cultivating communities of practice: A guide to managing knowledge.* Cambridge, MA: Harvard Business School Press.

Chapter 8

From Theory to Practice ... and to YOU!

Regardless of the role that each of us has in our higher education institution, information and literature certainly plays some part in our work. For our learners, accessing and understanding information and literature is central to their quest to becoming an expert in their chosen area of study. Many readers of this chapter might be involved in the generation of new information and literature through their research endeavours. For other readers, it might be about the protection, display, and sharing of information and literature (e.g., library, IT services, built environment). This "information and literature" takes on many forms and formats (e.g., course related materials, books in the library, open access books and papers, grey literature, audio productions, visual imagery, performance and art). However, this information and literature can be useless and obsolete if it is not generated and presented in a format that is accessible and engaging for the intended audience. As you can probably guess at this point, we will use this chapter to help us to think about – and more importantly, reconsider – why a UDL approach could be useful in making information and literature accessible to as many end users as possible from the get-go!

There is a key difference between higher education and other educational settings. This fundamental difference relates to the very active relationship we have with information and literature – largely defined by the ambitions that we have to develop new works that will be read, thought about, written about, engaged with, discussed, and debated. Increasingly, our attention is being directed towards ensuring that we democratise knowledge, through open access publishing and repositories, and also through international agreements to recognise that information and literature should be highly accessible and present a cause for action – for example, UN Sustainable Development Goals 4 and 10 (Quality Education and Reducing Inequality). Whilst each and every one of us can likely see how our work makes a contribution to the development of scholarly work, it is also likely that we have not, as yet, paid full attention to how we can ensure that this work is accessible to as many people in society as possible. That is, to what extent do we really consider the end user? To what extent do we really plan for the dissemination of our new information and

DOI: 10.4324/9781003137672-9

literature? Do we really consider, before the production of these new works, how they might need to be presented for a wide audience? As noted throughout this book, the philosophy and practice of UD and UDL (e.g., Multiple Means of Representation) can (and should) be a first thought, rather than an after-thought. And so, in a reflexive manner, it is important for each of us to recon-sider our relationship with information and literature in our jobs.

Everything in Life Is Becoming Easier ... But Not Yet Automatic!

Stop for a moment and imagine the routine household job of doing the laundry. Not so very long ago, perhaps for our parents' generation, this was an arduous and physical task. For us, we now have the luxury of having sophisti-cated machines that can make the task so much simpler. Anyone (well, most of us!) can follow the directions on the washing machine, load it up, select a program, and activate the start button. Simple. Quite straightforward. Until that one pink sock plays havoc with your whites!

From this example, we can see that we rely quite a lot on cognitive shortcuts to help us with many of the routine tasks of our life, operating for large amounts of time on automatic pilot, divided attention, and heuristics. This is a normal part of human life. We are limited in our capacity to process all of the information that our senses are continually receiving. In an interesting analogy, we are "cognitive misers" (Fiske & Taylor, 1991, seeking cognitive shortcuts where we can. Just as a miser looks for opportunities to avoid spending money, the human mind also looks for opportunities to avoid spending cognitive and thinking resources. How much attention do you really pay when you last crossed the road or travelled to work? Were you on auto-pilot, working on divided attention, and doing more than one thing at a time? Whilst this enables us all to move through our day and daily tasks quite quickly, the downside is that we can become lazy and ignorant of possible solutions to novel tasks, resorting to old stereotypical ways of doing things. It prevents us from explor-ing new approaches. We tend to favour information and approaches that confirm our long-held beliefs and behaviour patterns.

And so, whilst we know that UD and UDL can make our work tasks easier, they are not automatic (yet!). As cognitive misers, we need to accept that we have these very normal, and very productive, biases. We need to adjust our thinking, mindset, and approach to our work tasks – the ones that we currently do all of the time, and the new ones that we are planning for. As highlighted in Chapter 7, a Community of Practice approach could be useful here – gently challenging each other and the assumptions that we have been making about our work – with a particular focus on information and literature. We need to slow down, rethink the task, and be open to the new approaches that UD and UDL can provide. By not doing this, we will be neither reflexive nor creative and imaginative.

Everything we do requires a little planning and thought. Active inclusion efforts and UD/ UDL are no different. To be successful, we have to think about what we are doing and why we are doing it. Regardless of whether or not we appreciate the potential of UD and UDL, the reality is that changes in work practices and wider society are already taking place. We all like "win-win" situations. If you have to develop or make some changes to information and literature in your work, doing so with some purposeful intention results not just in getting the job done but in getting a job done that has been designed from the "get-go" to be as inclusive and accessible to as many people as possible.

How many of us have actually stopped to consider whether our information and literature is accessible? Most of us have probably just considered information accessibility in terms of whether a learner who is blind/visually impaired can access the information and literature with screen reader software. For researchers, they might consider accessibility to be about the democratisation of knowledge through open access. How many of us stop and think about how our learners relate to the information and literature that frames so much of our pedagogy? And, subsequently, how they might then apply it in their work and professional practice?

In many of our higher education institutions, we prepare learners for the world of professional practice, much of which involves work with – and for – the wide diversity of individuals that represent society. If we expect our graduates to be able to demonstrate active inclusion and UD/UDL thinking and practice in their professional work, then this begs the question: how could they do this if they have not seen it modelled in their courses and wider higher education experiences? Also, much of the content in these courses is focused on the application of "theory to practice". Perhaps it is also time for us to truly consider the application of "practice to theory". After all, information and literature will also be central to the work of these graduates. Are barriers to successful practice and client engagement akin to the medical model – whereby the problem is viewed as a deficit in the client being able to engage in the work and support of the professional? Or, from a social model perspective, perhaps the client experiences such issues and problems with engagement by the very fact that the presentation of the information and literature serves to disable their participation? To enact such change can be easy. When we design and redesign courses, it can be easy to orientate the course learning outcomes to "the WOW Factor" – that is, "the World of Work Factor". If we have this embedded at the course level, then it is rather easy to have this "WOW Factor" established in the learning outcomes for each module and each learning-related activity.

In this chapter, we explore the connections across our varied work tasks in higher education. We encourage you to reflect on your current and planned work activity, and consider the influence and impact that information and literature can have for the variety of learners and colleagues that we serve. Considering that information and literature are central and fundamental components of what everyone in higher education does, this chapter asks if you can see easy and sustainable "wins" for your work in enhancing active inclusion and accessibility.

The Role of the Librarian ... and Everyone Else

When we first think about information and literature in a higher education setting, our thoughts are never too far away from the role of the librarian. Whilst the librarian and their expertise is important to our discussion, we also need to accept that these colleagues do not stand alone as the gatekeepers to accessible information. Each and every one of us has a role to play. However, we often find that some of our teaching and research colleagues do not believe that they have any active role to play in the development of a more inclusive institution. But, through their thinking, reading, planning, analyses, and dissemination activities, it should be fairly obvious that the teaching and research community in our institutions have a fundamental role to play in the active inclusion conversation. Decisions made by these colleagues in their work, individually and collectively, can have a great impact on enabling access to information and literature – whether for course-related readings and supporting activities, or for the dissemination of research across a wide variety of publications, platforms, or events.

In relation to research, for example, whilst there might be some form of quality assurance in terms of the research process (e.g., funding applications and funder requirements, ethics applications and ethics committees, standards for literature reviews and data analyses, peer review and editorial boards), there is generally no attention as to whether the research project was inclusive (e.g., following UD/UDL principles). In recent years, there has been (rightly) more focus on ensuring that publicly funded research is made available, free of charge, to everyone in society. However, there is often far less interest or attention as to whether or not the finished product (the research itself) is accessible to the greatest majority of people – that is people both inside and outside the specialist area under investigation. In the absence of such thinking or action, what we see is continued exclusionary thinking and behaviours. Whilst this might not be the intention, and be completely innocent and inadvertent, the outcome is still the same. And so, how can we all advocate for greater UDL-led inclusion in our institutions and the information and literature that we both use and generate? Scholastic information is power, and history has taught us that we need to appreciate and respect this power.

The Librarian

In the previous section, we mentioned the highly important role of the librarian. As "information and literature" is a broad topic, it is useful at this point to pause and reflect on some work that one of our colleagues has done in this area.

Geraldine Fitzgerald is a Subject Librarian for the School of Education and the School of Psychology at Trinity College Dublin, Ireland. Prior to working in Trinity, Geraldine worked in a number of special, corporate, and academic libraries in Ireland and Sweden. Geraldine is passionate about improving the user experience of learners and has developed a number of digital resources, including tutorials and floor plans to aid wayfinding. Geraldine reflects upon a recent active inclusion project that she has been involved in – the TCD Sense project (https://www.tcd.ie/disability/services/tcdsense.php) to improve the library sensory environment.

Geraldine Fitzgerald, Subject Librarian

"Libraries have a reputation for being a safe and welcoming space, providing accessible information, and delivering free and equitable community programs and services" (Petropoulos, Banfield, Obermeyer & McKinnell, 2022). Today, myself and colleagues keep noticing that the increasing diversity of learners on our campus means that we need to rethink our more traditional approaches in the library.

While we continually aim to engage with all learners on campus, we noticed that one group having low usage was a group of learners with intellectual disabilities. These learners were undertaking an internationally innovative two-year full-time education and work-readiness course called "Certificate in Arts, Science and Inclusive Applied Practice" (https://www.tcd.ie/education/courses/arts-science-and-inclusive-applied-practice/). We decided to explore how we might improve the university library experience for these learners.

Having engaged in similar library projects, we wanted to include these learners in a real and meaningful way. We valued their user experience, and so we invited them to be our co-researchers in a participatory research project. The project vision was a library where future learners with intellectual disabilities could believe that the university library was their library and a space they could use more often – particularly when studying for exams, working on assignments, or even as a place to take a break.

The learners agreed to be involved and decided that a video recording of their experience when using the library would be a very useful tool. An ethics application setting out the project, the gap that it would fill, what it would involve, and who would be involved, was completed and approved. The research team included the librarians together with learners with intellectual disabilities. This was most important so that all were actively engaged in all stages of the project, whether setting out the project for an ethics committee or the research team, onboarding participants in an informed and inclusive manner, or disseminating and actioning the project outputs. Importantly, these learners had experience of UDL in action. Their course was heavily influenced by UDL thinking and practice. So, as "experts by experience", there was much that we could all learn from their observations and thinking about the project.

A key activity for the project was the focus groups which were organised to explore the learners' relationships with the library. This involved a reflection as to how their college library might be different to other libraries and just how it contributed to their experience on campus. They pictured different situations in the library – for example, asking for help or borrowing a book, and teased out challenges and barriers that they faced.

Common themes around "library anxiety" (Mellon, 2015) emerged from the research project:

- **Complicated buildings and not knowing how to find your way around** (e.g., confusing signs, physical layout including tall bookshelves, crowded spaces, and so much information);
- Knowing who library staff were and **how to ask for help** – very often there is a fear around asking for assistance;
- **Using library machines** (e.g., catalogues and book borrowing) – many learners revert to Amazon or Google Scholar rather getting assistance to learn how to use the library system;
- Fear of setting off the **security alarms**;
- Not feeling part of the **library community**;
- Autistic learners in the group experienced **sensory overload** due to their extra sensitivity to lighting and noise levels;
- Concerns around **personal space** was also identified;
- The idea that the college library could be a **social space** was considered a contradiction, because the idea of the traditional library, where the emphasis was on silence, predominated.

This research experience contributed to a video and also a greater recognition with regard to improving library accessibility for other learners. The video story, the draft roles, scripts, and timetabling for the shoot were created by both the learners and the library staff.

Consideration was given to every aspect of information being developed – recognising that this output could be a useful resource across the campus. While the video, as an information tool, was very welcome, other factors were also identified as a consequence of the project:

1 Creating more **visual communication** – videos using plain language, more visual based library brochures, and visual website information that can be easily navigated;

2 **Developing situated learning experiences** – a demonstration of typical library tasks (e.g., entering / exiting the library with ID cards, using catalogues, asking for help, borrowing on machines or at the desk) helps to normalise and familiarise these new situations;

3 An **increased awareness of sensory overload** – future learners need to know in advance where to find quiet, private study spaces so they are not concerned about noise and personal space. Sharing information about the Assistive Technology Information Centre (ATIC) on the video using an actor was also considered to be of benefit;

4 Designing a **welcome video** – the video particularly focused on learners and their interactions with staff and friends, showcasing the library as a "social space";

5 **A library is for more than books** – librarians shared the range of material available to students, including the DVDs and other material that may not have been thought of previously.

Most interestingly, there has been a steady ripple effect from the project for real and positive change across the library for inclusion. Many of these new developments have their roots in UD and UDL thinking. Library improvements continue to be reappraised, including more flexible borrowing rights, appropriate library signage, 3D floorplans on the website, sensory surveys of both library and university spaces, better staff awareness and relations with a growing diversity of students, task-based library training, and regular contact between librarians and learners seeking inclusion in the library and all that it holds.

And finally, co-authoring an academic paper with the project learners was a very tangible and sustainable contribution (see Fitzgerald, Dunne, Biddulph, O'Donovan, O'Rourke, Ryan, McGilton, O'Rourke, & O'Callaghan, 2020).

From my involvement in this project, I have been able to see how case studies such as these can be extrapolated to the larger student population. For example, I have since been involved in a cross-departmental initiative, the TCDSense project, which aims to improve the sensory experiences of students and staff on campus. I have also consolidated my understanding of UDL in the field with more formal learning by completing the Trinity Inclusive Curriculum module for Teaching and Learning (https://www.tcd.ie/equality/projects/inclusive-curriculum/).

In her role as Subject Librarian for the School of Education, Geraldine is always aware of the reading lists that are constructed for the various courses and when she sees a new topic that looks interesting, she updates some of her own thinking. Whilst she was already aware of the debates about disability (e.g., medical model versus social model), Geraldine saw the UDL readings as a useful personal learning goal and identified a potential tool for her own work. At first glance, the concept of UDL and the examples of practice are rather obvious, intuitive and even exciting. Geraldine successfully applied some UDL in her own work. We all have great opportunities in our work to update our own knowledge and thinking. While Geraldine's main role as a librarian is related to how we manage our information and literature, making it available for our learners and colleagues who need it for research and teaching tasks, her learners, the borrowers, are all humans. As is evident from her case, Geraldine really appreciates that each borrower has their own approach, and sometimes difficulties, in accessing this information and literature. Geraldine was able to learn from her involvement in a college project – personally and professionally. She was able to update her knowledge and practice of UDL, becoming more confident in "having-a-go", and listening to the learners who had an intellectual disability.

From Geraldine's reflections, we can see that engaging with UDL really is a reflexive journey – both personally and professionally – and not simply a destination. As noted earlier, we often hear colleagues proudly report that they have "UDL'd" it! Geraldine is still on the journey, seeking new opportunities to learn and practice. UDL does not have to be an arduous journey. To paraphrase Confucius, we need to remember that "the person who moves a mountain begins by carrying away small stones".

In Geraldine's work, a large part of the focus is upon managing and making information and literature available. However, we need to also move back a step in the process and encourage those amongst us who develop this new information and literature to be mindful of UDL and create our work in a manner that is considerate of the end user "from the get-go". Before we put pen to paper, we need to consider how we can adopt an inclusive approach in our thinking, writing, and publishing. It is important that the process of developing knowledge moves beyond basic and cursory considerations about physical and electronic access to new information and literature for a diversity of people. New UDL inspired approaches need to transcend the current outmoded approaches. In the absence of seeking new approaches to share information and literature, there will remain a distinct lack of proper engagement and discourse with the diversity of individuals that make up our society.

The Hairy Lemon Pub!

For anyone who will listen, Conor has three mantras that guide his writing. He keeps repeating these to his research students – who sometimes pretend to listen! In each of these, Conor has gradually embedded more of the components of UDL thinking. At the outset, there was no direct UDL input in any of them. Rather, they just seemed intuitive and were useful approaches in Conor's work. This is something that we often find in UDL practice – an approach that seems intuitive yet reflects some of what a UDL approach would advise. That is, Conor had developed approaches that had some UDL components "by accident, rather than by design". In knowing that UDL needs to planned "from the get-go", Conor has reflected on these mantras and has attempted to continually embed UDL thinking into each of them.

Each of the mantras stems from one very basic fact – that the English Alphabet consists of only 26 letters. In our primary school education, once we learnt how to write these letters in lower-case and upper-case formats, we learnt about how these letters can be easily put together in different configurations to become words. We also learnt that these words can be added together in a meaningful way to make sentences. Then we learnt that sometimes we need commas and full stops. To cap this learning, we learnt about putting sentences together to make paragraphs that can tell a story. None of these words were beyond the reach of our childhood understanding. Importantly, the adults who were helping us with homework and practice understood the words and what we were trying to convey in our stories. For Conor, the question becomes: "How hard can it be to generate easily accessible new information and literature from the various amalgamations of these letters?" Also, why do many researchers and writers try to make their writing complex, confusing, and full of "big words" that nobody really uses in everyday life? Is it that they feel that they need to do this to seem smart or intelligent? Whilst we might have our Seamus Heaneys and Stephen Kings, why do so many academics and researchers feel that they need to punctuate their writing with fancy styles and approaches that are not authentic?

In the first of his mantras, Conor reflects on the quote that is attributed to Ernest Hemmingway: "There is nothing to writing. All you do is sit down at a typewriter and bleed." Conor's interpretation and use of this quote is to reinforce the message that writing is not as easy as many people think it is. Many readers only ever see the finished product – the information and literature that was crafted through multiple drafts and reworking of the words and narrative. Good writers consider, from the get-go, the audience, and that the words and narrative must resonate and be meaningful to the reader. They also have to be accessible. We have all had experience of trying to learn from a book that was not well written, only to find a different book that could easily convey what we needed to know. There was probably a common and fatal misunderstanding on the part of the first author – writing in a manner that was personally pleasing and satisfying – with no real understanding as to how, you, the reader would engage with the writing. Thus, good writing requires attention to UDL thinking. Like any new skill, this requires practice.

For the second mantra, Conor reflects on the fact that many early-stage researchers report that they can easily write at least 1,000 new words each day, and that the thesis will be finished quite easily. Whilst this might actually be true for some gifted researchers and writers, it is often the case that this is a fallacy. Like the Hemmingway quote, these confident and boastful utterances often demonstrate a naivety about good writing. For anyone who will listen, Conor will happily confide that he would be the happiest writer in the world if he could write 50 good words every day. This is often met with a few giggles and a few questions about the truth of it. However, when you think about it, Conor said 50 "good" words "every" day. That is, whilst it might be easy to write a lot more that 50 words, the question arises as to whether these are good words – well thought-out, pondered, considered, tried, written, edited, and so on. The second part was about the ability to do this consistently – every day. It is not as easy as it first appears! Slowing down the process and reflecting upon UDL components and guidelines will ultimately result in a better offering.

And so, to the Hairy Lemon pub we go for the final mantra. For those readers not familiar with Dublin (Ireland), it is easy to navigate the city and its suburbs by the names of its famous pubs. Whilst in other cities, this might be done by street names and important road junctions, directions in Dublin will often start with a question about whether you know where a certain pub is (e.g., The Hairy Lemon). From that, it is easy to then see if you know where a different pub is (e.g., The Bleeding Horse, The Stag's Head, The Yellow House, Johnnie Fox's, The Foggy Dew, The Brazen Head, The Temple Bar, The Long Hall, The Ginger Man, The Gravediggers), and this helps to understand the general geographic direction of where you need to navigate to.

In this mantra, the two central components are navigating and communicating. This is no different in the development of new information and literature. To emphasise the importance of this, Conor often asks the student to think about (in their mind) going to the Hairy Lemon pub with Conor and his mum. Conor poses the following scenario:

> If I were to go to the bar to get drinks for the three of us, and you were left behind at the table with Mrs Mc Guckin, would you be able to communicate your thinking and project details with Mrs Mc Guckin? Would you be able to do this in a manner that is interesting for Mrs Mc Guckin and brings her along your "story" in a simple and straightforward manner? You would have to remember that whilst Mrs Mc Guckin might have a Ph.D. in your subject area, it might also be the case that she has no education experience beyond the basic schooling that she received when she was young. Would you be able to present your story in simple and easy sentences? Would you be able to gradually take Mrs Mc Guckin on the journey whilst not losing the essence and important detail of the research? The overarching tasks here are to provide directions and to communicate, making sure that you do not upset Mrs Mc Guckin or make her feel stupid. After all, you wouldn't want to upset Conor or Mrs Mc Guckin, would you? If you communicate in this manner, and if Mrs Mc Guckin then tells you that she has a Ph.D. in your subject area and has a Nobel Prize for her efforts, then it is easy to "step on the gas" and increase the technicality and speed of the communication. Can you see UDL components at work in this mantra?

It's More Than Language

In this chapter, we have started to consider the importance of the librarian in the custodianship of the "family silver" – the information and literature that is so fundamental to the working of a higher education institution. We have also started to consider the role of the academic and researcher in relation to the development and dissemination of new information and literature. In both of these examples, the centrality of UDL thinking and practice has been evident. For active inclusion to be beneficial for everyone in the higher education community, there is a fundamental need for reflexive practice and subsequent planning, at both a personal and a professional level, to ensure that what we do is both open and inclusive. When we consider information and literature, we can now see that the language and words chosen can serve to inadvertently exclude, and even negate, the experience of some learners.

Even in terms of these very basic issues about information and literature, many of our higher education institutions are notorious for being obscure in their use of language, sustaining some form of mystique about their hallowed halls, and very few are just confident enough to present written information in "plain English". In many of our own areas of expertise in higher education, there always appears to be a tried-and-trusted approach to how information is produced and made available. In our own institution, commencement ceremonies (i.e., graduation ceremonies) are still held in Latin. Whilst there can be something romantic and nostalgic about everyone being in gowns (each communicating certain information about the wearer) and the orator making pronouncements in Latin, it is not a very accessible event. Regardless of the attire and the issues that come with that, for all we know, the orator could be reading the sports results! Even the building that the commencements are held in is so old that there was never any need for the designer to incorporate ramp access to facilitate access to the building, the gallery, or the stage where the award is made. At best, we now see a metal ramp appended to the steps outside for access via wheelchair or for those who prefer not to have to use the steps. Like so many old buildings and ways of doing things, there was never any need for such access to be provided, because people with disabilities were never viewed as people who should be included. Similarly, allowing access to collected works of material is what most of our institutions are about – and very often this can be unashamedly elitist.

The Fallacy of the Average Learner

Despite the obvious diversity and variability to be found amongst our learners, the curriculum (e.g., learning goals, learning outcomes, teaching methodologies, media/materials, and assessments used to support learning [Assessment *for* Learning, Assessment *of* Learning]) is often designed and implemented for the imaginary "average" learner (Rose & Meyer, 2006). This concept of the average learner is just as much a fallacy as the notion of the anthropometrically "average person" (Daniels & Churchill, 1952; Robinette & Mc Conville, 1981). The fatal flaw in this approach is the premise that a "fair" curriculum is one whereby every learner is learning in the same way (Meyer, Rose, & Gordon, 2014). Implementation of a narrow and inflexible curriculum that targets the "average" learner comes at the expense of supporting all learners well but is especially unfair for learners with diverse backgrounds or who have differences in their abilities to learn. When learners are paired with an inflexible curriculum, the variability found in learners is often perceived as a challenge that must be overcome through remediation of the learner.

A UDL approach helps educators to understand how inflexible curricula are the problem, not the learner (Gordon, Gravel, & Schifter, 2009; McGuire, Scott, & Shaw, 2006). Instead of seeing the variability of learners as being a challenge to overcome, UDL encourages educators to ask: "Is the curriculum designed to optimise learning for all learners?" Asking this simple yet critical question shifts the focus from viewing variability in the learner as the problem to recognising that it is the curriculum and learning environment that needs to be fixed (Meo, 2008). In a similar vein, a UDL approach helps us to identify that the literature we engage with and use to support our teaching needs to be considered, as learners embrace new challenges in society today.

Celebrating "Individual Differences"

As identified in the field of psychology "individual differences" are those big issues at the centre of being human – for example, intelligence, personality, motivation. If we accept that everyone is uniquely different in their psychological makeup, then it makes no sense to design learning environments or rely on literature and information for only one type of individual. Rather, we should recognise and celebrate the fact that, as individuals, we each have our own unique and idiosyncratic thoughts, feelings, and interests. And moreover, each of us is likely to have some additional learning requirement and a plethora of different experiences prior to, or during, our engagement in learning. What is without doubt is that each of us will experience, at some time in our life, either a temporary or a long-lasting impediment to our ability to learn. Indeed, we all relate to the information and literature that we read and engage with differently.

UDL originated with this in mind, just as UD before it did. At its essence, a UD/UDL approach seeks to create a system that appreciates individual differences and experiences. As noted in earlier chapters, the medical model of disability has often sought to define disabled people by their medical condition (Borsay, 2006). This deficit approach focuses on both the loss and the need for medical intervention, seeking to "fix" the individual so that they will "fit" with our idea of "average" or "normal". In essence, this approach individualises the "problem" and transforms a description of a condition into a description of people. Consider the language that has been associated with the medical model – words like "disable" (dis-able) and "invalid" (in-valid) are negative in connotation and meaning. Whilst we might be upset by this type of language used to describe fellow citizens, we also need to remember that many of us who have studied psychology probably participated in a module called "abnormal psychology". This is reminiscent of the anti-psychiatry movement of the 1960s and the views of Thomas Szasz and R. D. Laing (among others), who proposed that mental ill health and psychiatric issues would be better understood in terms of the person having "problems of living", rather than as a need for a medicalised and pharmacological approach to helping the person.

The COVID-19 pandemic resulted in learning activities across higher education moving swiftly online. A request to participate in learning online or to record a lecture was once an onerous process, with numerous steps needing to be successfully navigated (e.g., meeting with a course tutor and probably the Disability Officer, medical verification, needs assessments, approval, check with university and college protocols). Within a week, most learning activities were moved online and recording facilitated. The new norm had arrived. A new world experience demanded that our engagement be redesigned. For many, the impossible was suddenly possible. Whilst these changes to higher education have been beneficial for many, we also need to recognise that they have presented barriers for other learners (and colleagues).

If we are to follow the advice attributed to Winston Churchill, we should "never let a good crisis go to waste". From our UD and UDL perspective, we need to now consider how we can learn from our Covid-19 experiences. In terms of information and literature, what should our engagement with colleagues and learners look like? Will we recognise that there are individual differences in the choices that we have to make – for example, some colleagues might prefer to attend meetings in person, whilst others might like to join online. Or, will we revert to approaches that only please the majority? Will we actively reflect on these changes and evolve our thinking and action from previous ingrained approaches and "habits"? In many ways, this raises the question as to who can and should be included. Who requires a different approach? And, a more delicate question, who has the power to decide?

Designing for Individual Difference with a Collective "Mindset"

When designing for inclusion with UDL, we need to think like a true designer, considering both form and function. In relation to information and literature, rather than just enabling a learner with a disability to participate on an equal basis with their peers through the provision of reasonable accommodations (e.g., adapted text/video/audio options, extra resource hours, access to a Special Needs Assistant, assistive technology), UDL demands we take a step back and redesign the whole learning environment, so that the end result becomes useful for a universality of learners.

UDL requires us to look afresh at learners and recognise that each one has a diversity of human experience. Each learner has their own unique approach to their learning and the information and literature related materials that they need to engage with. UDL should be the antithesis of a checklist approach to teaching, learning, and assessment issues. Such approaches become a "tick the box" exercise, routinised and actionable without any real need to think beyond the question posed in the checklist. Individual differences amongst us all demonstrates that we each have preferences for how we wish to access information and literature. For example, for any of us that reads novels for pleasure or relaxation, we can make the choice of engaging with the novel in a hardback format. Others among us might prefer to read the novel in a soft cover format, finding the hard covers to be just too awkward and clumsy to manipulate when holding the book. Audio versions of the book can be a great choice if we wish to listen to the novel being read to us when we are walking or travelling. Quite often, we might have the opportunity to watch a dramatisation of the novel on television, in the cinema, as a theatrical production, or downloaded as a video file to be viewed at a time convenient to us. In audio and video formats, we can listen or view at normal speed or multiples of normal speed – the choice is ours!

Ultimately, each of us has these "multiple means" of accessing the same information and literature, with some of us choosing more than one form of engagement.

When we engage with the seven principles of UD, we always remember that whilst these were originally developed to guide architects and designers in relation to their work to design inclusive buildings and products, we need to interpret them for application to our own practice. Outside of their original use, many of us use these seven guiding principles "as a yardstick rather than as a template". That is, we do not need to see them as proscriptive. We can use them as guides for our work – subtly translated for our own needs and requirements. In a similar manner, we need to remember that the UDL framework and its principles and guidelines were originally designed for teachers. Whilst some of us will see immediate applications of the UDL framework to our activities at work, others among us should similarly see these as useful yardsticks for thinking and action. The beauty here is that we can use UD and UDL as "thinking tools", actively seeking opportunities to develop proactive and retroactive solutions to enhance the higher education experience for our learners, out colleagues, and ourselves! The UD and UDL framework give us the permission to "rethink" our needs and wants. When we consider the relationship between individual differences and information and literature, we can see the appeal of a UD and UDL approach. Each of can identify with the broadness of the learning experience, and with how we have personal preferences for accessing and engaging with information and literature. After all, we are all life-long learners who wish to be successful in our efforts.

Connecting with Practice

In this next case example, Dr Gloria Kirwan shares with us some of her ongoing personal and professional reflections about her work and how emerging UDL thinking about information and literature is starting to have an impact. Gloria is a leading professional Social Worker and Senior Lecturer at the Royal College of Surgeons in Ireland (RCSI). Gloria is the co-editor of the advanced and contemporary thinking included in the *Routledge Handbook of Digital Social Work*. Throughout her career, Gloria has become highly influential, demonstrating quality leadership in terms of reflecting upon where the discipline has been, and importantly, where it needs to be in terms of being positioned appropriately to provide suitable services to clients in an ever-changing society. What is particularly useful about Gloria's reflections is that even though she is highly experienced in the professional and academic fields, as a reflexive practitioner, Gloria recounts how her developing interest and knowledge of UDL has enabled her to see new opportunities for the increasing importance of UDL in digital social work. There is an important convergence of theory and practice (or practice and theory) in this example.

Dr Gloria Kirwan – Professional Social Worker and Senior Lecturer

In my thinking and practice, I am guided by the following important definition from the World Health Organization (2002, p. 10) regarding "community participation":

> a process by which people are enabled to become actively and genuinely involved in defining the issues of concern to them, in making decisions about factors that affect their lives, in formulating and implementing policies, in planning, developing and delivering services and in taking action to achieve change.

Participation in education and society is about empowerment. Empowerment has been defined as "... any process whereby those lacking, comparatively, in power become or are helped to become more powerful" (Pierson & Thomas, 2002). Similarly, Peter Beresford (1999) associates empowerment with liberation and with being in control of one's life. The antithesis of empowerment is the deficit-focused characterisation of certain groups in society (Kennedy Chapin, 1995), and the paternalism underpinning service systems designed to make best-interests decisions about individuals, as opposed to informed decisions led by individuals when they need help and support.

With the increasing influence of digital technologies, UD and UDL have the power to truly manifest an inclusive society. Enacted within a social work environment, there is very real potential to supercharge the empowerment and participation of marginalised sections of society (Kirwan, 2022). We are all participants in the social welfare system. For some of us, we might have experiences of this being less than inclusive – being clunky and too standardised to account for any small difference that our circumstances might need. Whilst we all have an aspiration for a more inclusive society, ongoing research findings and new developments mean that we are seeing the development of a digitalised social welfare system.

In my work, I have been reflecting on what these new developments will likely mean – for me, for the profession, and for all of the various clients that we seek to support in our work. I have been fortunate to have been exposed to the utility of UDL in a higher education setting. The various components of UDL theory (e.g., multiple means of representation) have challenged, yet encouraged, me to consider what UDL might be able to do if utilised in social work approaches. For example, I have challenged myself to reflect and consider if all of the issues that we encounter with clients could actually be mitigated – or removed completely – if we had alternative means to engage with service users (e.g., the forms that we use, our approaches to meetings) and also alternative methods for our clients to communicate with us.

In my work as an educator in higher education, I have witnessed the transition from a "medical model" of how we understand our learners who have additional requirements in their learning, towards a more inclusive, equitable, and "social" model of support. Much of what we do in our higher education work continues to be influenced by the ongoing influence of the digital revolution. A similar transition is happening in my professional work, with "digital social work" (see López Peláez & Kirwan, forthcoming) presenting new opportunities for people to live independently and participate on their own terms in the wider society. The potential of UD approaches to reduce exclusion and dependency and improve the individual's independent participation in society has been understood for some time (e.g., Article 2 of the United Nations Convention on the Rights of Persons with Disabilities [CRPD] (2018). The report of the 11th session of the CRPD (2004) goes on to state that

> without access to information and communication, persons with disabilities cannot enjoy freedom of thought and expression and many other basic rights and freedoms ... New technologies can be used to promote the full and equal participation of persons with disabilities in society, but only if they are designed and produced in a way that ensures their accessibility. https://www.ohchr.org/Documents/HRBodies/CRPD/GC/DGCArticle9.doc

Thus, whilst UD is recognised as a useful element in the design and delivery of empowering and participative ICT services, its applicability in many activities and spheres remains undiscovered, under-acknowledged, or not fully understood. UD and UDL are not concepts that are prominent in the educational curricula of the various social professions that qualify people to deliver the range of social services.

Also, with some exceptions, UD and UDL have not been prominent topics central to the discussion regarding the development of digitalised resources in the social welfare field.

In my work, we need to develop confidence in our competencies to lead on these new developments. We can learn from what has been attained in education. Whilst the ICT developers of new digitalised approaches will likely adhere to all of the UD principles, and other design standards, it is the task for myself and my colleagues to ensure that our UDL knowledge can be translated into something useful for our "learners" (i.e., our clients). There is, it seems, a lot to do but much to gain.

Central to Gloria's reflections are issues related to information and literacy – both in their current and well-trodden formats – but also in terms of how we need to rethink these issues as we move further towards digitally mediated relationships and work patterns. While contemplating the digital journey ahead, it is useful to be reminded of an early but currently very relevant observation by Ron Mace, where he reflected upon the overall benefit of UD:

> Early on, advocates of barrier-free design and architectural accessibility recognised the legal, economic, and social power of a concept that addressed the common needs of people with and without disabilities. As architects began to wrestle with the implementation of standards, it became apparent that segregated accessible features were "special, more expensive, and usually ugly. It also became apparent that many of the environmental changes needed to accommodate people with disabilities actually benefited everyone".
>
> (Story et al., 1998, p. 19)

Rethinking and Reframing Exclusionary Practice

As we have noted throughout the book, a central component in the conversation about UDL has to be the internal dialogue and reflection that each of us needs to engage in. We all need to appreciate that each of us has a unique understanding as to what we mean by inclusion as it relates – and influences – our own work. We seek to move from silo thinking of each man for himself towards a "wheels of inclusion" approach – where the learning and experience of UDL is always moving and developing, connecting us all, while seeking to improve the learner experience.

The learner experience is deeply rooted in the teaching, learning, and assessment activities related to course participation, together with the information and prescribed literature we engage with. As we consider who is challenged by access to the written word, it can be easy (and lazy) to just consider those individuals who have a print disability or visual impairment. But, having reviewed the case examples provided by Geraldine, Gloria, and Conor, perhaps we need to view this in a broader manner, and realise that when it comes to accessing and producing the literature that informs our teaching and learning experiences, a wide range of issues can impact on this process.

The development of and access to "information" and literature has always been a key theme for education. Reading and writing have over time been considered the two main competencies necessary for access to learning, but is our understanding of how people learn evolving? The digital age is changing our learning environments and our engagement with literature – perhaps even our literacy.

The key when considering "inclusion" is to reflect on what scholarship "was", "is", and "can be" while also reflecting on this as we develop our thinking for the future. Our research activities, as we engage on this journey, also need to reflect this process.

Academics at all stages in all schools across the campus never rest! They seek to find the new and add it to the knowledge that has gone before. At all stages we seek to influence – and build an argument. We use what we are learning to create new learning and so positively or negatively influence the lives of children, parents, families, communities, policy, and practice. Should we choose to ignore "UDL", we will limit future learning and understanding – not just about inclusion – but for the very learners we do and will engage with.

What Are My Learning Goals?

As you progress on this learning journey it is important to reflect and ask, how can you infect the literature and practice in your field? And moreover, how are you affected *by* the literature in your field? Are you adopting a position of reflexivity – reflexivity is "active" and is more than reflection. Are you changing? How are you changing?

UDL as a design concept demands change. It is not enough that we adopt inclusion because it looks nice! Think about the last time you planned a holiday! You possibly went online and engaged on a travel website – but did you choose a destination just because it looked nice and the photos were good? Or did you stop first and think about what you wanted from your holiday, plan what to bring and who to bring, tease out whether you would like sun or snow, active or relaxation, somewhere near or far. Did you next consult with others – professional and friends – had they been? What did they think? Did you read the reviews? How much did all this influence your thinking? Did you re-evaluate what you wanted from this lovely holiday as you researched – engaged with other websites and people – as you read the text and looked at the pictures? You were actively considering all your options as you browsed through the information you accessed. There was a time when you would just pick up a holiday brochure, flick through the pages, consult with the travel agent and make a choice. When we think about this – it feels so limited – doesn't it?

Can we learn from our engagement with information that shapes our everyday living? As we engage on a journey of discovery about inclusion – do we also need to reconsider our relationship, actively and ethically, with our research? How do we as researchers adopt a UDL approach? In "Inclusion as Process" (Quirke, Mc Guckin, & McCarthy, 2022) the authors ask, "why would you expect the world to keep changing if you, yourself, are not also changing?"

Conclusion

Much of the thinking about inclusion is siloed by virtue of the group of people it serves – often keeping the discourse separate and quiet and focused on a reactive rather than proactive approach. UDL demands a multidisciplinary and interdisciplinary approach, just as UD did. It is not just for teachers and disability, nor can it be. If that is the case – it has failed. It needs to grow and boldly take on the shared agenda of inclusion so many seek to advocate for. It will in turn generate new literature and a new literacy about inclusion. A shared discourse that will seek to emancipate so many who know what it is to be excluded.

Simply put – as academics – we need to stop, think, and share.

Points to Consider

Take a moment to reflect on your own subject area – how had you considered UDL in relation to your work (your teaching, learning, and scholarship) in this area up until now?

Reflect as to how does this chapter sits with you. Does it challenge you or sit very comfortable with you?

One of the challenges of UDL is that it is more than just applying a set of guidelines in our classrooms, rather it is about exploring our deeper assumptions and unconscious bias regarding inclusion in and for higher education. Moreover, it will also demand that you explore how your scholarship brings value to professional practice, future research, and future learners. Take a moment to consider:

What ideas or values does UDL rely on?
How do these relate to my discipline and work?
What is my reaction to this?
How might I react differently?
What feels most comfortable and best for me to do right now – as I seek to affect my work?

References

Petropoulos, J.-A., Banfield, L., Obermeyer, E., & McKinnell, J. (2022). Contextualizing inclusivity in terms of language: Distinguishing librarians from "library staff". *Journal of Library Administration, 62*(4), 535–556. DOI: 10.1080/01930826.2022.2057131

Beresford, P. (1999). Towards an empowering social work practice: Learning from service users and their movements. In W. Shera & L. M. Wells (Eds.), *Empowerment practice in social work: Developing richer conceptual foundations* (pp. 259–277). Toronto: Canadian Scholars' Press.

Borsay, A. (2006). Personal trouble or public issue? Towards a model of policy for people with physical and mental disabilities. In L. Barton (Ed.), *Overcoming disabling barriers: 18 years of Disability & Society* (pp. 161–178). London: Routledge.

Daniels, G. S. & Churchill, E. (1952). *The "average man"? WCRD-TN-53-7.* Aero Medical Lab, Wright Air Development Center, Wright-Patterson Air Force Base, Ohio.

Fiske, S. T., & Taylor, S. E. (1991). *Social cognition* (2nd ed.). New York: McGraw-Hill.

Fitzgerald, G., Dunne, S., Biddulph, N., O'Donovan, M-A., O'Rourke, M., Ryan, S., McGilton, S., O'Rourke, D., & O'Callaghan, H. (2020). Improving the university library experience of students with intellectual disabilities: A case study from an Irish institution. *Disability & Society, 35*(10), 1698–1704. doi: 10.1080/09687599.2020.1781597

Gordon, D. T., Gravel, J. W., & Schifter, L. A. (Eds.). (2009). *A policy reader in Universal Design for Learning.* Cambridge, MA: Harvard Education Press.

Kennedy Chapin, R. (1995). Social policy development: The strengths perspective. *Social Work, 40*(4), 506–514. https://doi.org/10.1093/sw/40.4.506

Kirwan, G. (2022). Manifesting an inclusive society: Using universal design theory with ICT to supercharge the empowerment and participation of marginalised populations. In A. López Peláez, S. Mok Suh, & S. Zelenev (Eds.), *Digital transformation and social well-being: Promoting an inclusive society* (pp. 61–67). London, UK: Routledge.

López Peláez, A. & Kirwan, G. (Eds.). (forthcoming). *Routledge handbook of digital social work.* London: Routledge.

McGuire, J. M., Scott, S. S., & Shaw, S. F. (2006). Universal design and its applications in educational environments. *Remedial and Special Education, 27*(3), 166–175. https://doi.org/10.1177/074193250602700305

Mellon, C. A. (2015). Library anxiety: A grounded theory and its development. *College & Research Libraries, 76*(3), 276–282. https://doi.org/10.5860/crl.76.3.268

Meo, G. (2008). Curriculum planning for all learners: Applying universal design for learning (UDL) to a high school reading comprehension program. *Preventing School Failure, 52*(2), 21–30. https://doi.org/10.3200/PSFL.52.2.21-30

Meyer, A., Rose, D. H., & Gordon, D. (2014). *Universal design for learning: Theory and practice.* Boston, MA: CAST Professional Publishing.

Pierson, J., & Thomas, M. (2002). *Collins dictionary of social work.* London: Collins.

Quirke, M., Mc Guckin, C., & McCarthy, P. (2022). How to adopt an "inclusion as process" approach and navigate ethical challenges in research. In *SAGE research methods cases*. London, United Kingdom: SAGE Publications, Ltd. https://doi.org/10.4135/9781529605341

Robinette, K. M., & Mc Conville, J. T. (1981). An alternative To percentile models. SAE technical paper 810217. Warrendale, PA: Society of Automotive Engineers. https://doi.org/10.4271/810217

Rose, D. H., & Meyer, A. (Eds.). (2006). *A practical reader in universal design for learning*. Cambridge, MA: Harvard Education Press.

Story, M. F., Mueller, J. L., & Mace, R. L. (1998). *The universal design file: Designing for people of all ages and abilities*. Revised Edition. Retrieved from: https://files.eric.ed.gov/fulltext/ED460554.pdf

United Nations Convention on the Rights of Persons with Disabilities (CRPD) (2018). Report of the eleventh session of the Conference of States Parties to the Convention on the Rights of Persons with Disabilities. Retrieved from: https://documents-dds-ny.un.org/doc/UNDOC/GEN/N18/244/06/PDF/N1824406.pdf?OpenElement

World Health Organization, Regional Office for Europe (2002). *Community participation in local health and sustainable development: Approaches and techniques*. Copenhagen: World Health Organization.

Chapter 9

Adopting the Right Attitude on the New Universally Designed Campus

Many colleagues involved in higher education believe that they already take a UDL approach to their work, not particularly recognising that UDL is in any way a new concept or something different to what they already know or practice. Many of us are already involved, somehow, in campus initiatives related to "widening participation" or "equality, diversity, and inclusion". In continuing to develop our own personal and professional thinking and action regarding this work, we can work to encourage a new model for active inclusion that will highlight and ameliorate the insidious effects of exclusion, leading to campuses and work activities that are truly about access, diversity, and equality. In this chapter, having engaged with this book and reflected on the different experiences our colleagues are having with UDL, we ask you to consider the question: how do we make UDL a shared philosophy and practice that we can adopt, together?

Education matters. It matters for individuals and for society. It is only in recent times that higher education has become more attainable for the diversity of individuals and groups who are representative of society. Education is much broader than the topic matter of lectures, seminars, laboratory practicals, field trips, and participation in clubs and societies. The United Nations' Sustainable Development Goals implore us all to develop "Quality Education" (Goal 4) and "Reduce Inequality" (Goal 10). Our own institution has identified four Graduate Attributes that learners are expected to demonstrate upon graduation: to act responsibly, to develop continuously, to think independently, and to communicate effectively. For the contemporary workplace, such highly and widely educated learners are increasingly required as we move further towards a knowledge economy.

Indeed, as many colleagues often say, we are educating learners for jobs and careers that do not yet exist. The world is continually changing, and it is not just the job market that reflects these changes. The opinions, views, and norms of society are in continual flux. The needs and desires of citizens are changing too. Higher education can no longer be a cold house for individuals or groups who have traditionally been excluded from our institutions. As our campuses

DOI: 10.4324/9781003137672-10

become more representative of the diversity of society, we continually need to consider whether we are challenging ourselves enough to check on our assumptions, prejudicial thoughts, and possible discriminatory actions. As we have noted, many colleagues are already doing something in their work that could be a useful reflection of the philosophy and practice of UD and UDL. In many of the instances, these examples of great practice have happened by chance. The trick for everyone now is to enact UD and UDL with intention – "having-a-go-from-the-get-go" (Quirke & McCarthy, 2020).

Inclusion Interrupted

As we began our work on this book, the Covid-19 pandemic unfolded, resulting in challenges and changes to every part of our institutions and our work. What was considered initially as a transient intrusion resulted in significant interruption to daily life on campus. With the necessary closure of our physical campuses, teaching and learning activities moved quickly online. We all know that there have been different types of engagement, with some being more successful than others. Whilst the complete focus was upon increasing accessibility, this was not achieved for every learner. Unfortunately, much of the thinking about how to pivot and move teaching activities online disenfranchised many learners. As usual, the learner population was seen as a homogenous set of individuals, with a "one size fits all" approach often enacted. We acknowledge that understanding and latitude was usually provided "after the event" for learners who experienced difficulties with the new approaches to engagement. What was well demonstrated through these activities was that the diversity of the learner population was either not understood or not acknowledged. At a basic level, the move to online assumed that every learner would have access to uninterrupted and high speed broadband, and that they would have a laptop or tablet that could be used for study. There was no real appreciation or understanding of digital poverty. Nor was there any real consideration that learners who were parents might need to make their hardware available for their children who were also having to complete school work from home. In essence, changes resulted in exclusion for the first time. And, this was not solely for our learners. Many colleagues had to assume other important caring duties whilst at home. Everyone suddenly needed to have a workspace at home. Unacknowledged was the fact that not everyone had a home, or had the luxury of having a quiet office space. Many non-academic colleagues had never been trusted to have a laptop and the opportunity to work remotely, being required to travel long distances to sit at a desk and complete work tasks that could easily be done at home or at a location of their choosing – just like their academic colleagues. Initial considerations were focused on how to engage, how to find new ways of doing things, and how to develop new ways to learn. As time has progressed, there has been the realisation that the Covid-19 disruption is not going away.

The idea of permanent exclusion, with the possibility of being side-lined and being left behind, has become very real for many learners.

Of course, the Covid-19 pandemic has not been the only driver of world change. Across recent years, we have witnessed the emergence of many new, and globally important, issues. All of these have the same central message – the need for inclusive thinking and action. Globalisation and macro level issue are felt acutely at the local and micro levels. Recent global issues (e.g., climate change, wars, energy prices, new diseases) have all had the ability to have direct and immediate impacts on our lives, our families, and on how we engage with each other and understand learning and work. Such chrono-system (e.g., Urie Bronfenbrenner) changes are felt and experienced at a personal level. They can have long-lasting reverberations – like the ongoing reverberations of a drum once it has been struck with a drumstick. For many of us, we have all had feelings of isolation, feeling impotent to effect change, or disabled by the way in which society has been organised.

Inclusion matters. Inclusion has always mattered. Inclusion is not a new concept, and as we have argued, needs to be considered in its widest definition, and not simply as being about disability or extending what we already do in relation to disability to other work practices and learner supports. The recent Covid-19 pandemic has not highlighted so many new issues for higher education rather, it has simply thrown a spotlight on issues that were always there, either obviously so or latent in the system that they remained ignored, because there was no real will to either acknowledge or address them.

As the world continues to change, both within and outside our campuses, a new seed of active inclusion is emerging. It is the responsibility of each and every one of us to reflect upon this, to adapt our current work practices and, critically, also our assumptions about our learners. As a design for action paradigm, it is apparent that UD and UDL offer us a contemporary framework from which we can reconsider inclusion. UD and UDL present an opportunity to redesign and do what we do best.

Pulling It All Together

In this book we have explored a contemporary approach to ensuring inclusion in learning environments: UDL. Throughout history, there have been many individuals and groups who have experienced exclusion in both education and society. To exemplify this, we explored the experience of people with disabilities. As a group, people with disabilities were, arguably, the first of these excluded groups to be considered in terms of inclusive educational and societal practice. Political engagement and focused advocacy resulted in changes to theory, policy, and practice. From this work, UD emerged as a catalyst for change in the built environment and the design of products. The success of UD was translated into action for educational environments through the CAST approach to UDL.

Whilst each of these developments happened at the macro level, we also set out how experiences of both exclusion and inclusion can be highly personal for individuals and their families (i.e., at the micro level). Our argument is that "inclusion is everybody's business" (McCarthy et al., 2019) and that we can no longer see the job of "inclusion" as being for someone else in our institutions. Mc Guckin and O'Síoráin (2021) have made similar arguments for early years educators and school teachers, emphasising that we all have a role to play in including our learners. Indeed, Mc Guckin and O'Síoráin (2021) encourage us to "stop and stand and stare" – to take the time to slow down – to reflect and consider our work and the importance of what we do for all of our learners.

Each and every one of us has our own experience of feeling excluded. We all have our own struggles. The difference is that some of us struggle more than others, and context matters very much. Indeed, to link directly back to the issue of disability, it can be a very sobering thought for anyone who does not have a disability to acknowledge that each and every one of us will experience either a temporary or a permanent disability at some point in our life. And so, from a selfish perspective, our ongoing personal engagement with being reflexive practitioners will enable us to continually change our own hearts and minds, and the hearts and minds of others, to create learning and living environments that will be inclusive of our own additional requirements when the need arises.

Take a moment to think about how you manage your time. Do you have too little time to do and achieve the things you want to do? Maybe you have too much time and are challenged to find things to fill your time with? Are you challenged by strict deadlines and a lot of demand on your time, having to creatively balance time between work and home life? Think of one situation where managing your time is a challenge, and take a moment to consider what you do to cope. Does allowing 10 minutes extra to travel or reach your destination help? Or perhaps a new "to-do" list? Or maybe even reaching out and asking for assistance? The key message here is that we all struggle, and moreover, we all have coping strategies. Sometimes our struggle is common and similar to the experiences of others. Yet what we do to manage the situation might be very different. Or perhaps our solutions can be shared, as they might work for others also. Struggling is part of the human condition. This is not to undermine the significant challenges faced by many amongst us, but rather to highlight that we need to shift our thinking to a place where inclusion, as framed by UD and UDL, is a shared opportunity, rather than a shared problem.

Living History: How the Past Can Frame Our Thinking

Historically, education was often segregated with explicit barriers to learning. This exclusion and segregation is still very relevant for many of our learners today. As we reflect upon past experiences, it is important that we are mindful of the present experiences of so many.

As noted, whilst educational and social exclusion was not unique to people who had a disability, new thinking and action challenged us to consider what was acceptable and what could and should be done to generate change. Much has been captured and described in the literature about the experiences of people with disabilities, and the push away from segregationist thinking towards a more social model of how we can include and support learners with additional needs and/or disabilities in education. These developments supported the development of UD and UDL – approaches that could move beyond disability and take a universality approach, focusing on shared experiences of limitation and exclusion to create opportunities for inclusion.

The application of UD thinking and the core principles developed by Mace and colleagues to education has been evidenced in different approaches, models, and frameworks that were outlined in Chapter 3 (e.g., UDL, UID, UDE). We often get asked by colleagues, which of these approaches is the best? In response, we encourage these colleagues to see each of the approaches as thinking and action tools, and like any tools, that it is better to have a toolbox approach rather than a hammer! We pose the question: if you invited a handyperson around to your home to fix a radiator, would you be happy if they turned up with only a hammer? Rhetorically, we ask if the handyperson will fix the radiator with the hammer. Of course, this leads to the obvious discussion that whilst the handyperson might try to fix the radiator with the hammer, it is the wrong tool for the job, and the outcome will be a botched job. We finally agree that it would be preferable if the handyperson arrived with a toolbox, one that has many tools in it, and from where the handyperson might choose the right tool for the job – a wrench. Similarly, we encourage our colleagues to think about the approaches using the "3 C's". That is, whilst each of these approaches will have obvious areas of "comparability" and "contrast", we should see them as being able to "co-exist" in our toolbox, providing us with a broader and deeper appreciation of the issues, and how these tools in our inclusion toolbox can be used interchangeably to create learning and work environments that are inclusive for the great diversity that we see among our learners and colleagues. Regardless of similarities in terms of nomenclature, each of the approaches outlined in Chapter 3 share the same goal – to redesign for inclusion in learning environments. We have a lot to learn from these UD and UDL trailblazers.

The CAST model of UDL has become the most identifiable approach for so many people in education, most notably at secondary school level. The CAST model has been conceptualised and continually developed from knowledge and empirical evidence from the fields of neuroscience, psychology, and education. Placing the learner experience at the centre of its philosophy, the CAST framework and guidelines are easily understood and easily applied to learning environments. For anyone new to UDL, the CAST approach provides a rich source of thinking and guidance for planning work in an inclusive manner, from the very start of the planning process.

Moving Beyond Disability

The use of UDL in higher education continues to develop, with many new initiatives seeing the application of UDL thinking to much more than the traditional issues of teaching, learning, and assessment. With such increases in inclusive practice, targeted at the universality of our learner population, the role of the Disability Service and the Disability Officer is changing. Historically, the Disability Service had a focus on one-to-one supports for the small number of learners who had a disability. As UDL becomes more embedded across all aspects of higher education, there are new demands for the support and knowledge of the Disability Service. In a positive move, the role of the Disability Service is changing. The remit in terms of active inclusion is now larger and wider than disability.

Central to each of the UD and UDL approaches is the ability to change and evolve in our practice, adopting a mindset that seeks to take a more dynamic and reflexive approach to inclusion. That is, rather than simply reacting and responding to situations that might exclude some learners as they arise, a proactive UDL approach will mitigate a lot of potential issues that could arise for our learners. So, as you reflect upon the different approaches and experiences of UDL in higher education, whilst also recognising your own personal and professional experiences, you should become more confident in developing your UDL competence.

It is evident that as UDL tilts the lens of inclusion and responsibility, traditional approaches to our work will change and new Communities of Practice will develop. UDL shifts our thinking about inclusion to new considerations about how we can strive for better inclusive learning environments and experiences. Such work demands both an individual and a community approach. Our colleagues who have contributed to this book have reflected this approach, sharing their own UDL and inclusion journeys, noting that whilst they have begun their journey of reflection and action, they are not expert yet!

Ways of Working a UDL Attitude – The Power of U!

The greatest challenge that we all face as we move forwards with our UDL work is to ensure that we do not get lazy and slip backwards to old engrained habits, or to an approach whereby we see our UDL work as a simple "tick the box" exercise. Such approaches will quickly become limiting, being over reliant on add-on supports. The greatest challenge with UDL is that it is never done. It needs reflection before action. It always has to be intentional. It also needs constant vigilance and confidence to evaluate whether our new approaches are working. This is what a UDL attitude needs to be! We can all take comfort in the advice from the great Irish Nobel laureate Samuel Beckett about "having-a-go": "Ever tried. Ever failed. No matter. Try again. Fail again. Fail better" (1983, p. 7).

From the outset of this book we wanted to share the "attitude" necessary to promote UDL and inclusion across higher education. To this end, as we shared the experiences of some of our colleagues, we also hope we addressed some of the more common concerns and thinking we engage with, as a new approach emerges:

Is this an actual theory or a new practice?
Is it a bit of a fad, unproved and unscientific? How do I know it works – it's risky isn't it?!
How is it relevant to my work?
Aren't I doing it anyhow?

We hope that together with our colleagues we have answered some of the challenges we all face. What is perhaps more significant and worth noting is that "the conversation regarding inclusion" in education is changing.

The change asks that we listen and engage, and be most aware of our own position and our bias, and in addition – join in the conversation. An additional principle for UD or UDL would be **The Power of U** – what you know, have experienced, and appreciate in relation to inclusion in education, is what frames your attitude to UDL. As we reflect on our colleagues in this book, and so many others, the common space is their power and belief in relation to inclusion on campus; their attitude; their power.

Time after Time: Adopting a UDL Attitude

Throughout the book, we have explored how UDL presents us with new opportunities in both individual and shared work. We have considered UDL as something that is for everyone in higher education, not just those amongst us who have direct learner-facing roles. We have reflected upon the importance of active inclusion and the need that each of us has for feeling respected for our own unique individual differences. For our learners, and increasingly for ourselves and our colleagues, our work takes place in so many places and spaces – often wherever our mind sees fit! Learning is often a personal endeavour. Achievement can be highly personal. So too can our work in supporting our learners. In starting to adopt a UDL attitude, perhaps take some time to reflect upon these three steps:

Step 1. Think from a Place of Empathy – Think with Care

Reframe your approach with understanding. Recognise that your learners are intersectional and have a myriad of experiences and goals. Be aware of what has likely framed their thinking. Similarly, be aware of what has framed your own thinking. Understanding these elements is important in reflecting upon how shared thinking can shape our approaches and experiences in learning. Time waits for nobody – other inclusionary practices are already becoming dated. UDL thinking and practice is increasing and has the potential to be always contemporary, with its focus on all aspects of the higher education experience. There are new and emerging uses of UDL every day. These are widening and enriching the UDL discourse. For the ever-changing world that we live in, there always seem to be new issues and concerns for our learners to contend with. For us too, we are continually confronted with how to re-evaluate what we do, and whether our old and trusted approaches still hold any currency for the diversity of learners that we meet – and the diversity of issues that they encounter as they navigate the modern world. UDL presents a thinking and action approach that makes our work easier.

Step 2. Think from a Place of "Opportunity" – Design!

This is our time! This is YOUR time! This is the opportunity to revise and redevelop your approach to your work and consider how UDL might help you to make positive changes for inclusion. Even a small change could have a huge impact on a range of learners. We all aspire to a higher education system and wider society that are truly inclusive and respectful of each and every one of us. Inclusive higher education can be attained if we all take on the challenge and change our thinking and work practices. We can all make a modest contribution to the achievement of the UN's Sustainable Development Goals – especially Gola 4 (Quality Education) and Goal 10 (Reducing Inequality). Why not have a go! Why not encourage a colleague to join you and develop a small Community of Practice!

Step 3. Take the Time – And Be Open to Change, Engage!

A new UDL attitude demands that we make connections! We need to work across our institutions and their service areas, schools, departments, and faculties. There is no one quick fix. Different approaches and solutions are likely needed for our colleagues who work in different areas of the institution than we do. If the goal is to create a high-quality inclusive learning environment, then we need to be aware of the differing levels of individual learner support that might be required. This should be framed by individual requirements rather than by a disability. UDL does not negate the need for add-on support. Rather, it demands that it is:

- Responsive: aware of the different times that support might be required for different people;
- Intuitive: grouped according to need;
- Personal: available where and when necessary, support can still be individual and personal.

This is no doubt that this can be a balancing act, one that requires you to collaborate with your colleagues and wider community. And, importantly, this community includes your learners.

We quite often find that colleagues who are involved in inclusion initiatives expect that their work will makes positive changes to everyone and everything that was included in the project plan. Interesting, however, is the fact that these colleagues do not always seem to consider that they, themselves, should also change as part of the process. For us, we wonder how it is possible to be involved in active inclusion initiatives and not, through personal and professional reflection, be open to change. The following three steps can be useful in this work (Quirke, Mc Guckin, & McCarthy, 2022):

1 Think with care:
   i   Appreciate your own understanding of inclusion;
   ii Adopt an ethical approach.
2 Design to last – adopt and appreciate a reflexive inclusive approach:
   i   Design for inclusive engagement;
   ii Acknowledge challenges as they arise;
   iii Recognise "exclusion";
   iv Continuously rethink and redesign for inclusion.
3 Take time to engage with others:
   i   Appreciate relationships in the broader ecology.

The Way Forward

UDL is evolving as a concept that prompts educationalists to consider "designing for inclusion" from the get-go. As an evolving concept, with definitions and guidelines that are generally understood, if it is to be true to its ethos, it must frame professional practice across education systems, including higher education.

While it is often thought that the utopia of such a concept will lead to no supports or special services, this is not the case. UDL does not negate the need for support or add-on accommodation, nor does it necessarily lessen it. It just changes and will continue to change where and how need is identified and addressed. In truth – UDL takes an all-encompassing approach, recognising that as we engage with it we need to learn how to include as well as acknowledging the need to be included. This is the beauty of UDL – it does not allow hierarchy and redistributes the power in the learning relationship. As we move forward we need to respect our power and how we use it.

While the world outside reshapes education and learning, UDL offers each of us the opportunity to reshape inclusion and respond in a harmonious way with change as it occurs. This is a process that is dynamic, active, and evolving. UDL is itself being redesigned into a New Universal Design Education (NUDE) approach. By this we mean that a fresh new approach for inclusion is emerging as we "strip back to basics" of universality, designing, and inclusion and recalibrate in the context of contemporary higher education. Adopting approaches that work "well enough" but don't quite fit will not serve current learners or indeed the learners of tomorrow well. We now need an approach that is mindful, responsive, reflexive, and actively engaged for both you and your colleagues and the learners on campus this approach needs to "work for".

As you adopt this more dynamic thinking for inclusion, we hope that you can recognise what it has to offer and embrace it as an opportunity to really appreciate an inclusive approach that benefits everyone. Such thinking will ensure that all feel they belong; such approaches will be "factored" into our activities and scholarship as we go forward seeking a "gold-standard" inclusive campus.

What Do We Want Our Campus's to Look Like?

There are greater challenges for our world than ever before and not just to adopt new ways of teaching, researching, and learning in higher education. The greatest challenge of all is to ensure inclusion – that no one is left behind, be they learner, teacher, or researcher, in our rapidly evolving world of higher education. This is no longer a simplistic approach of adapting or considering access for a few – rather it necessitates a more sophisticated understanding as to what inclusion is and how UDL enables us to pivot both our thinking and practice.

The world of learning changed dramatically with Covid-19. Up to that time, inclusion was of interest, while it was on the edge – more so targeted at particular populations. Not everyone believed it to be their business and felt that some change was perhaps unnecessary or undoable, and opted out. A pandemic, the like of which has not been experienced in this lifetime, shifted the thinking around inclusion. Everyone had to redesign their engagement with not just their learners but their colleagues and their work including their research. What was most interesting is that many felt "excluded" for the first time – and can now identify with the feelings of being left out, left behind, or even disregarded. It is important that we all believe we can be part of the future learning environs – and this shifts the design focus onto an environment all seek to engage in.

A UDL attitude offers a doable concept that can be adopted in so many different ways across the higher education system. This book has argued that it is a concept not just for the classroom, where its application had previously been confined to in the main – rather it is a philosophy and practice that can be adopted by the wider system, where each of us are important players.

What Does It Take to Do It Well? A Universal (University) Approach, of Course!

Irrespective of its origins, UDL does not belong to any one group of learners, nor is it an approach that is just applicable to one specific faculty. It is a theory that begs for an interdisciplinary and multidisciplinary approach. Appreciating and knowing how to design for inclusion can be challenging – especially as it is not as simple as a tick the box approach when education and all it demands keeps changing. The first thing we all must do is to reconsider our "position". **The Power of U**, as outlined earlier, is in essence your positionality and reflexivity in relation to "inclusion" – this exercise is something that is part and parcel of life in higher education. However, UDL is also about sharing and engaging!

The second step is to identify those who would be most useful for you, on campus – those also engaged in this thinking. They do not have to be in your school or department. And you may need to think outside the box! Search within, search without, and engage. Engaging on such a journey is best done with others and demands interdisciplinary and multidisciplinary relationships – just as any good design process does. It begs for a universality of thinkers and doers.

What may also come as a surprise to many is that engaging in "universality" means that we need to leave behind outdated approaches reflecting "silo" mentalities or approaches (e.g., that's not my department, we do things differently here). This approach does not rely on the pronouncements of experts, or those that have maybe been (arbitrarily) appointed to lead on a particular inclusion initiative (e.g., develop a Community of Practice), but certainly does rely on having a growth mindset (rather than a fixed mindset).

The very concept of UDL welcomes new thinking and new approaches. It will test what we know about inclusion as it seeks to encompass all ages, all stages, and all people. UDL is about acknowledging the myriad of individual differences that make us unique, and seeks ways in which we can make alterations to established practices to enable learners to demonstrate their full learning and potential.

What Might Get in the Way?

Time, of course! UDL is about designing and redesigning our thinking and action. Is this not what the academy is best at? Is it not our role to question received wisdom, from wherever or whomever it emanates? Is it not our role to explore, design, find answers, and push the boundaries of knowledge and applied practice? But this will take time, time to reflect, consider, critically think, and re-evaluate.

As you stop and reflect on what you know, consider where you might find further information or support to develop your knowledge, competencies, and confidence with inclusion and UDL. Lack of information is a challenge for some areas – while this is actively changing.

Ego can also get in the way! Recognise that UDL is all about the very best of what it is to be human – being able to lead, but also about being able to follow. It is not a fixed or set process – it is a responsive approach that demands constant re-evaluation and decision making. What works for one group of learners may not work for another.

Too narrow a focus. The discourse has to develop beyond the topic of disability into a deeper and wider focus for the diversity that exists within and between the very people we live with, work with, and learn with. Importantly, it is not just about one population – there is no hierarchy of inclusion. If we seek to include one person before another, or favour one group above a different group, we are "othering". We are being prejudicial in our thoughts and discriminatory in on our actions. Just like Lady Justice, we should remain blindfolded, and be impartial in our UDL work. A UDL approach should be applied without regard to whether it is individual circumstances, group membership, or other status. Always consider who you wish to actively include, ensuring that you are not limited to one audience.

Lack of clarity around key terms. The term "inclusion" is represented across different literatures and has resulted in different terminologies and discourses, which has presented a challenge in that some of the thinking about inclusion remains disjointed. UDL offers the opportunity to join up these past conversations and learning, bringing forward a new language and new terminologies, with a fresh appreciation as to how active inclusion might be defined.

Take a Developmental Perspective

UDL offers an opportunity to not just redesign how we include, but to redesign inclusion itself. Yet, as the world of learning continues to change and meet the pressures in our contemporary world, the origins of UDL, a world where people were excluded by design, must never be forgotten.

This is particularly evident with recent and ongoing learnings from the Covid-19 pandemic, as learning moved on and offline, engaging with new technologies and consequently redesigning curriculum and assessment, resulting in new and changing how people can be excluded. It almost felt like an inclusion roundabout – where you were lucky if you were on and not so lucky if you were left off or fell off. The funny thing was for the first time this analogy could apply irrespective of whether you were the professor or the student/learner!

So we must pose the question: should disability theory and "special inclusive education" lose its relevance, as a growing diversity of individuals need and want more from inclusion in learning today? Do traditional approaches to inclusion hold back the discourse? In short – no. But they are evolving and so too are our approaches. The approaches we espoused in the middle of the last century are very different to our thinking and approaches today. Our lives demand that we develop and re-evaluate our approaches for inclusion in learning, work and life. We can respect that the conversation is moving forward – as it should. But it is important that we do not forget the origins of the approaches as we adopt and adapt – or we will shift away from the ethos and spirit and we run the risk of excluding again.

Be Mindful of the Values Your Approach Espouses

Allow yourself time. Allow yourself to enjoy the change! Designing is supposed to be fun! Stop and think about the last time you followed a design project doing up a house on social media or on TV. Remember the stages involved, the planning, the deep consideration of wants and needs, the trials, the fails and the learning from them, more trials, the shopping or sourcing of necessary materials, the time it took and the support and engagement with a wide variety of people. The end result was a dream house! Designing is also a bit more than a checklist – while they are so helpful. Good design gives you the autonomy to consider need and to try out what you like – with support and encouragement. UDL is no different.

You are not alone on this journey. Respect *who* wants to be part of your UDL journey. Engage with colleagues and other professionals across the campus. Most importantly do not forget the learners themselves. In higher education, learning takes place in all of its spaces and places – learning in the undergraduate lecture hall, the lab, the library, the philosophical club – anywhere people gather and think. Online or offline. Learners in our academies engage in learning in so many contexts – and we must be mindful of that. Learning knows no boundaries. The real enemy here is to be that person who does not engage with learners. Even if you believe that UDL is not for you, someone else's job or just a fad that takes too much time, that is not good enough anymore. There is a diversity of people who want to learn, discover, understand, and achieve. And you need to engage and listen to their voice to allow that to happen.

The mistake, as an academic, when considering UDL, is to do nothing! Moreover, (don't tell everyone) but not considering UDL may be your greatest missed opportunity. We are living through great change and challenges for inclusion and exclusion. Every day people find themselves left out of discourse, cut out of conversations, written out of the literature, denied learning opportunity. As academics and learners, we need to continuously and mindfully reflect on how our landscape changes. Every day there is a new "excluded" in our environment and someone else is left out. Education is changing – so are our people. It is important that we, you, keep apace.

Conclusion

We started this book to share UDL and its thinking in its broadest sense while also communicating its appeal. UDL on the higher education campus does necessitate big thinkers and lots of thinking – however, it also allows for unlearning and relearning. UDL is not a fixed mindset, and anyone engaging in UDL needs room to breathe. It's a bit like stepping onto a moving escalator. It is a challenge the first time – everyone appears to be ahead, but once you are on you are also moving up! It is easy to be overwhelmed and worry about "getting it wrong" in a society that can be demanding and critical. But UDL is confident, encouraging, and progressive. UDL is all that we feel good about in learning – it is kind, authentic, and respectful, seeking to emancipate and encourage. It embraces those attributes we espouse across our democratic education system and in a true UDL environment, while there is no room for heroes, hierarchies, or privilege, there is always the time and space to engage understand and include others.

In conclusion we invite you to take the time to consider UDL as you develop your inclusive practice – consider it a shared opportunity. Make the time to develop your own UDL attitude – become part of the solution!

References

Beckett, S. (1983). *Worstward Ho*. London: John Calder Publications Ltd.

Mc Guckin, C., & O'Síoráin, C. A. (2021). The professional self and diverse learning needs. In S. Soan (Ed.), *What do teachers need to know about diverse learning needs? Strengthening professional identity and well-being* (pp. 15–32). London: Bloomsbury Academic. (ISBN: 9781350083196). Retrieved from: http://hdl.handle.net/2262/100285

McCarthy, P., Quirke, M., & Mc Guckin, C. (2019). *UDL – Can you see what I see ... is it an exclusive model or an inclusive model? Third Pan-Canadian Conference on Universal Design for Learning: Connecting the Dots – Sharing Promising Practices across Country*, 2nd–4th October, 2019, Royal Roads University, Victoria, Canada. Abstracts not published.

Quirke, M., Mc Guckin, C., & McCarthy, P. (2022). How to adopt an "inclusion as process" approach and navigate ethical challenges in research. In *SAGE Research Methods Cases*. London, United Kingdom: SAGE Publications, Ltd. DOI: 10.4135/9781529605341

Quirke, M., & McCarthy, P. (2020). *A conceptual framework of universal design for learning (UDL) for the Irish further education and training sector: Where inclusion is everybody's business*. Dublin, IE: SOLAS & AHEAD Ireland. Retrieved from: https://www.solas.ie/f/70398/x/b1aa8a51b6/a-conceptual-framework-of-univer-al-design-for-learning-udl-for-the-ir.pdf

Index

abnormal psychology 129
Access Office 66
Access Officer 68, 70
accountability 92, 110
action/expression, multiple means of 50, 56–59; executive functions 58–59; expression and communication 58; physical action 57–58
action-oriented approach 32
active inclusion 3, 4, 7, 9, 27, 31, 67, 71, 86, 88, 91, 119, 120, 139, 141, 147
add-on approach 38, 68
add-on thinking 20
ad-hoc approach 41, 75
affective neural networks 49, 50
affirmation model 6, 77, 79, 80
Ainsworth, M. 8
anti-ableism 93
antiracism 93, 94
Archer, C. 102–106
artificial intelligence 22
assistive technology 22, 35, 57, 69
Assistive Technology Information Centre (ATIC) 123
attachment theory 8
augmented reality 23
average learner, fallacy of 128
average person 19, 22, 24

Bandura, A. 8
Beckett, S. 144
Behling, K. T. 20, 23, 73
bias 92, 118
bio-ecology 112
Bourke, A. 36
Bowe. F. 37, 38
Bracken, S. 33–35
breaking down barriers 99–101

Bronfenbrenner, U. 8, 42, 112
Burgstahler, S. 34

Cambridge Centre for Teaching and Learning (CCTL) 81
capability approach model 6
Center for Applied Special Technology (CAST) 3, 29, 35, 36, 141, 143; action/expression, multiple means of 50, 56–59; applications 49; belonging and connecting with world of learning 62; engagement, multiple means of 49–52; naturally workable 66; pillars 49–59; recruiting interest 51; representation, multiple means of 50, 52–56; of UDL 47–64
Centre for Universal Design (CUD) 38
Chardin, M. 61
Charter, A. S. 30
childhood curriculum theory and practice 107
Children's Rights 107
chrono-system 141
Churchill, W. 130
City of Dublin Education and Training Board (CDETB) 102
cognition 7, 104
cognitive functioning 19
cognitive impairment 59
cognitive misers 118
cognitive psychology 55
collective efficacy (CE) 103, 106
Community of Practice (CoP) 73, 86, 98, 102–106, 118, 144, 146
Convention on the Rights of Persons with Disabilities (CRPD) 6, 133
Covid-19 pandemic 3, 21, 26, 30, 57, 71, 88, 95, 129, 141, 141, 148, 150

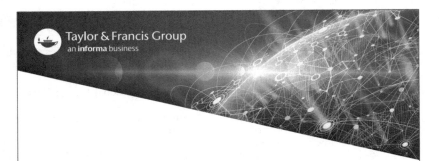